"I hadn't realized

how much I missed some things," Tina said.

"Like?" Adam asked, filling her glass again.

"Oh, the excitement of an opening, the taste of good champagne. Those aren't exactly a part of the daily grind at Timberline Inn."

"Tell me about your life out there," Adam said.

Tina hadn't meant for the conversation to get personal, but the questions Adam asked were intelligent, probing. He seemed to care about her life in the Rockies; he seemed to understand it. And that was what she found so strange coming from Adam Cole, who was, let's face it, a swinger. Yet she wasn't so naive that she couldn't detect the difference between a man who was making a play and one who was interested. Tina smiled to herself. Adam Cole was both.

Dear Reader,

When two people fall in love, the world is suddenly new and exciting, and it's that same excitement we bring to you in Silhouette Intimate Moments. These are stories with scope, with grandeur. These characters lead the lives we all dream of, and everything they do reflects the wonder of being in love.

Longer and more sensuous than most romances, Silhouette Intimate Moments novels take you away from everyday life and let you share the magic of love. Adventure, glamour, drama, even suspense— these are the passwords that let you into a world where love has a power beyond the ordinary, where the best authors in the field today create stories of love and commitment that will stay with you always.

In coming months look for novels by your favorite authors: Maura Seger, Parris Afton Bonds, Elizabeth Lowell and Erin St. Claire, to name just a few. And whenever you buy books, look for all the Silhouette Intimate Moments, love stories *for* today's women *by* today's women.

Leslie J. Wainger
Senior Editor
Silhouette Books

Images

Anna James

Silhouette Intimate Moments

Published by Silhouette Books New York

America's Publisher of Contemporary Romance

SILHOUETTE BOOKS
300 E. 42nd St., New York, N.Y. 10017

Copyright © 1986 by Shannon Harper and Madeline Porter

ISBN: 0-373-07135-3

First Silhouette Books printing March 1986

America's Publisher of Contemporary Romance

Printed in the U.S.A.

Silhouette Books by Anna James

Silhouette Intimate Moments

ANNA JAMES

spends most of her time in either Atlanta, Georgia, or Los Angeles, California. She has written many different kinds of romances—from historicals to contemporaries, as well as numerous Gothics. When she's not traveling or writing, she enjoys tennis, the theater, long walks on the beach and her three incompatible cats.

Chapter 1

The dining room at Timberline Inn was flooded with the bright sunshine of early morning in Colorado. Tina Lawrence Harris tied back her auburn hair with a dark blue cotton scarf, filled a big coffeepot and emerged from the kitchen. The heels of her run-down cowboy boots barely made a sound as she crossed the knotted-pine floor.

All the guests were up for breakfast, she observed, all seven of them. These were regulars, old faithfuls, whom Tina had known for years. She greeted them warmly and had just begun serving coffee when Eli Wicker hurried across the room, her slim figure slipping easily between the tables.

"Telephone for you," she told Tina. "It's New York calling." She said that last for everyone's ears. It wouldn't hurt to suggest that potential guests were making inquiries from the east.

"Finish up for me, Eli," Tina asked, handing her the coffeepot. "I'll try not to be long."

The response came in a whisper. "I think I can handle the crowd." Eli began to circulate among the tables. An elfin figure, she was part of the mountains she loved, and she couldn't understand why old-fashioned resorts like Timberline were slowly going out of fashion. She ached for Tina, who'd put herself so completely into the job of making Timberline a success. Even now, in early September, Eli knew that ski resorts all across Colorado were busy gearing up for the winter influx while Timberline barely held on to its faithful few. Sadly Eli watched Tina leave the dining room, cross the drafty hall and go into the cranny that served as her office.

Inside, Tina closed the door, collapsed in the worn leather chair and propped her feet on the desk before picking up the phone. The energetic voice on the other end of the line was familiar, a semimonthly voice that Tina had come to count on.

"So how are things in the frozen North?"

Tina grinned. "This isn't the North, Kay. Remember? It's the West, just your side of the continental divide, also called the Rocky Mountains. And we're not frozen yet. There's only a dusting of early September snow."

"Sounds bleak just the same. Here in New York we're just beginning to think about putting away our summer whites and bringing out the fall wardrobe. But I didn't call to talk fashion or weather. I called to talk about you, honey. Or rather, Bettina."

"Bettina is dead, Kay. Figuratively speaking," Tina added. "There's nothing for you to discuss with her. However, you could tell *me* all sorts of things—like what wonderful fall outfits you purchased at Bendel's this week?"

"How did you know—" Tina could visualize the look of confusion and then understanding on Kay Cooper's broad, country-bred face before she answered. "Stop guessing about my shopping sprees! It wasn't Bendel's, anyway; it was Bergdorf's. Now hear me out, Tina. I have the opportunity of a lifetime for you—for any model."

"I'm not a model, Kay," came the response. "We just went through that. I'm not Bettina anymore."

Kay ignored her. "Adam Cole, Century Cosmetics. Ring a bell?"

Tina pulled off the scarf and shook her hair loose. Breakfast was over. Eli had finished serving coffee, and the dining room would be clearing out. Tina leaned back in her office chair, the decision made to play along since Kay was determined to have her say— with Tina's cooperation or without it. "I've been out of modeling and away from New York for nine years, Kay, but I'm not living on another planet. Adam Cole is the head of Century Cosmetics."

"Okay, so you know about him, but do you know about Generations? Of course not," Kay answered her own question. "News is just breaking here. Generations, his new line, will offer cosmetics for every stage of a woman's life—from teenage to the middle years. They're mounting a promotion based on a mother-daughter concept—"

"And you want me for the daughter," Tina quipped, well aware of her friend's real agenda and suddenly anxious to avoid discussing it if possible. But distracting Kay once she had sunk her teeth into a topic was only slightly easier than disengaging a hungry dog from his bone.

"You look young, Tina, but let's not be ridiculous. The girl has been chosen. She's Holly Cole, Adam's fifteen-year-old daughter. Been modeling for years. Here's the amazing part, Tina: you and Holly look enough alike to be actual mother and daughter—the same hair, the same blue eyes, even the same skin tone. My God, it's uncanny. This job is made for your comeback."

Stubbornness finally crept into Tina's voice, replacing the earlier flippant tone. She swung her feet off the desk and leaned forward. "Comeback? Oh, no. I'm not about to—"

"Wait until you hear the offer before you say no. That's the first rule in any business, Tina. Remember when you didn't want to do those jewelry ads—"

"Kay..." Tina was getting irritated.

"And I finally talked you into them because of David Stern. I knew that through his photographs, still another image of Bettina would emerge. David always said you were a chameleon, remember?" Getting no response, Kay forged ahead. Shyness hadn't made her one of New York's top agents. "Well, this offer will knock you out. It's not an hourly fee, Tina. We're talking about a three-month campaign—TV, print, promotion—the works. A buy-out for more money than you ever dreamed of." Kay named a large sum, a figure that was almost obscene. "That kind of cool cash will take care of all the debts on old Timberlake—"

"Timberline," Tina corrected, still a little overwhelmed.

"Lake...line," Kay swept on, undaunted, "you could have that eighteenth-century kitchen redone and a new bathroom put in and the heating system updated..." Kay and her husband had spent a Christmas at the inn, buried under two feet of snow with the electricity out, and Kay was well aware of Timberline's aging facilities. She was equally aware of Tina's financial situation, which shifted from precarious to dangerous and back again with alarming regularity amid a dwindling clientele. "You could probably put in your own ski slope with that kind of money."

"Hardly," Tina answered. "Let's not get carried away."

Kay slowed down and breathed a sigh that carried from her New York penthouse to the mountains of Colorado. Then she allowed her voice to soften, losing its high-pressured sales pitch. "You were the best, Tina. The very best."

"You said it, Kay—*were*. Those days are over, and even if I wanted to come back, what makes you think that Adam Cole—or anyone else—would hire me?"

Kay heard the question and pounced on it. The *if* brought back her verve. "Fly here for the tests and let me handle everything else. A lot of time has passed, Tina. A lot of water over the dam."

"People remember..."

"Only what we want them to remember," Kay said confidently. "I'll handle that problem. You just show up—and look beautiful."

Tina saw where she'd been led and pulled back quickly. "Out of the question," she said, "I have the inn, responsibilities—"

"Tell you what," Kay countered. "I'll call you back tomorrow after you've had a chance to think about it,

to think about the money—and what it'll buy for
Timberline.''

"It's only a test, Kay."

"I can land it for you, Tina, so don't let me down,
honey.'' The line went dead.

Tina held on to the receiver, trying to organize her
thoughts. Her head was spinning with all of Kay's
ideas. None of them made any sense at all. Except the
amount of money she'd mentioned. Tina looked
around her cramped office. That money could certainly make a difference, but it was an unrealistic
dream. She wasn't going back; she couldn't go back.

Finally, Tina hung up the phone and slowly made
her way into the dining room. The guests had left their
tables, some wandering into the den to read the
morning papers, others sitting before a fire in the front
parlor and the more vigorous heading for the hiking
trails or the stables. It was a beautiful, crisp morning,
sunny and bright. On a day like today, the inn should
have been teeming with guests. But it was September,
and September could be unpredictable in Colorado.
Not many people were willing to take a chance on the
weather, and by late fall, when snow was assured,
they'd all head for the ski slopes. Tina sighed, picked
up a plate that Eli had missed and went into the
kitchen.

It *was* eighteenth century; Kay had been right about
that. But it was also warm and cozy with two big gas
stoves, a center chopping block over which heavy iron
pots and pans hung, plenty of counter space and an
industrial-sized refrigerator about to breathe its last.

Eli was loading the antiquated dishwasher. Tina sat
down on a bench by the long counter. ''That was Kay

Cooper," she announced, picking up a sponge and wiping off the counter top.

"I figured," Eli said. "Just gossip—or is she laying one on you again?"

"The latter," Tina answered with a smile. At least once a year, Kay made her futile plea. "She wants me to come back to New York for some tests. This time it's a little different. There's a lot of money involved, enough to put this place in shape."

Eli looked up, raising an eyebrow. "That *would* be a lot. What's the deal?"

"A new line for Century Cosmetics."

"Aha. The magnificent Adam Cole. Wow."

"Wow? That doesn't sound like Eli Wicker, the confirmed mountain girl. What do you know about the man?"

"He's in *People* magazine all the time—always with a different blonde on his arm. Divorced years ago...a confirmed jet-setter ever since—"

"Enough, enough. I didn't know you read anything lighter than the *Whole Earth Catalog*," Tina commented.

"I read magazines at the grocery store checkout counter. Kam and I always get in the longest line when we're shopping for the inn so we can catch up on all the gossip."

Kam, Eli's boyfriend, was the other half of the inn's second team. He served as chef, waiter, handyman and trailblazer, and he read history, listened to classical music and didn't even watch TV. Trying to visualize him at the magazine rack, Tina shook her head. "Well, it's not Adam Cole who interests me, anyway. It's the job. That is, it's the money."

"Go for it, I say."

"What about the inn?"

Eli closed the dishwasher door and turned the dial. The machine gave a couple of violent gasps before beginning a reluctant cycle. "At this point we need your money more than your presence, Tina. Kam and I can handle the overflow crowd of seven," she assured her.

"The Marshalls will be coming next week. You know, they like to ski but prefer lodging away from the slopes." Tina heaved a sigh and stood up. "Damn, if only that ski area over by Peaceful Valley had gotten past the planning stage, I wouldn't have to worry about making this decision."

"So you're seriously considering it?"

"Not really. Just thinking out loud. That part of my life is over. It ended when I married Bryant and left New York. It's a door that I slammed shut, and it's not likely to open for me again."

By the time the long day was over, the dinner dishes cleared away and loaded into the tired dishwasher, the fires lit and the tables set for morning, Tina had forgotten all about New York, Century Cosmetics and Adam Cole. Or if not forgotten, her thoughts were tucked away in a place that she hoped was permanent.

It wasn't. She found herself thinking about the money as she climbed the stairs to bed. The suite that she and Bryant had once shared was on the north side of Timberline and looked out on the ragged snow-capped peaks of the continental divide. The three large high-ceilinged rooms caught the worst of the wintry blasts of arctic wind. Even now in early September, a fire burned in the grate. With the disappearance of the sun in the Colorado Rockies, the nights were bitter seven months of the year, cold three months and cool the other two; and if there wasn't snow on the ground, it could be seen in the distant mountains *every* month with the possible exception of August.

Tina sank onto the big four-poster bed and pulled off her boots. Often the days seemed endless, and there was never enough time to get everything done. Yet if life was hard here in the mountains, it was also healthy and invigorating, and certainly it was straightforward. Here no one judged. Here, Tina could be herself, look her age, dress any way she pleased as long as she stayed warm. There was no pressure to be more than just another human being, no demands to reach for the top, the impossible.

Tina began to undress, pulling off her jeans and plaid shirt and slipping on a long nightgown. She caught a glimpse of her reflection in the mirror and moved across the room for a closer inspection. She stared at her image. Her eyes looked tired, and without makeup her cheeks lacked color except for a misleading flush from the fire. Tina attempted a smile. Actually, she wasn't bad for almost thirty-six, but she certainly didn't look like the exotic Bettina.

She'd managed to put Kay's plea aside during the long day and fill her time with work, but she hadn't really succeeded, for her friend's words had determinedly stuck with her, much like a cocklebur clinging to her jeans. Now that the day's work was over and the guests had all gone to their rooms and the night was quiet except for the crackling of the fire and an occasional howl of a coyote in the distance, she was left with time to think.

Tina wrapped herself in a warm robe, pulled on her fleece-lined slippers, sat back down on the bed and let herself wonder whether it would be possible to fit into that old life again. It was there, Bettina's life, high in a bookcase over the mantel. It was pressed into a faded blue scrapbook, and it hadn't been opened for years. Tina stared at it for a long time until it seemed to draw her off the bed, over to a stool by the fireplace, where she climbed up and reached for the scrapbook. Blowing off the dust, she sat in a big wing chair before the fire and put it on her lap, unopened.

She remembered the day she'd bought it, making a surreptitious trip to the store and pasting in the first picture that afternoon; a wide-eyed girl with her life planned. Tonight she felt the need to relive it. She turned to the first page and looked down at the newspaper clipping: Tina Lawrence, winner of a state beauty contest. How proud her parents had been of their only child, and how excited she'd been over that contest. Optimistic, a little naive, very determined, Tina had believed that with her title she could grab the world by the tail and spin it around.

Everything began the day after she won the contest, bought her scrapbook and left for New York with five hundred dollars in her purse and her parents' warnings ringing in her ears. She didn't look back, at least not while she was still young. Tina Lawrence, from Longmont, Colorado, had decided to become a model; not just any model, but the best. Now, so many years later, she smiled as much in sympathy as amusement at those youthful fantasies that, in one way, had come true; for a while she'd been at the top.

She turned the pages and looked at her first head sheets and composite photographs. She'd gone to New

York armed with a few color pictures, not knowing that she needed these glossy eight-by-tens, not even knowing what they were. She'd found out quickly. At her first interview a not so patient secretary had raised a thin eyebrow and asked to see her "book." Before the day ended, Tina was sitting in the office of the photographer that same secretary had grudgingly recommended.

Tina stared down at the first pictures David had taken of her. She'd kept the proof sheet, his orange grease-pencil marks still faint around the ones he'd chosen to print. She turned the page and traced the lines of an enlarged photo.

"Good cheekbones, high and prominent, full mouth, eyes wide apart, strong chin." The words of David Stern came back to her. She could see him plainly, sitting on a high stool, one elbow resting on his knee, one hand cupping his chin, scrutinizing her carefully and deciding, "You'll do." That was the *real* beginning.

Tina looked through the pages at David's other photographs taken that first day and in the weeks that followed. Hers was a face that his camera, any camera, loved, David had insisted. And he'd been right, even the imperfections, the little bump on the bridge of her nose, the space between her front teeth, the full bottom lip, turned into advantages, giving her face distinction.

Fortified with her "book," Tina still found the going rough as she trudged from agency to agency, getting no more than a few "cattle calls" to join mobs of other girls vying for television commercials.

"And that's what they are," she told David, "cattle calls. We march through one by one; they have a

look and see if we're right. I haven't been right yet,"
she added. "But my whole vocabulary is changing.
They also call that little parade, aptly enough, a 'look-
see.'"

"I know, darling," David said with a laugh. "But
you mustn't worry. As soon as you sign with a model
agency, you'll be on your way. No more cattle calls.
No more look-sees."

She signed just in the nick of time. When she was
down to her last twenty dollars, Tina made an appointment with a newly established agent, Kay Cooper. Kay had come to New York from Alabama, a big
rawboned country girl with sandy-colored hair, a wide
good-humored face and a ton of ambition. After
working for five years in an office job at one of the top
model agencies, Kay had struck out on her own and
settled herself in a very unglamorous office on a very
unfashionable street with half a dozen free-lance
models, two signed exclusively, and a staff of one—
herself—to make the bookings, interview the girls and
answer the phone.

The moment Tina walked through the door, Kay
knew the struggle was over—for both of them. She
took off her glasses, ran a large hand through her
sandy hair and admitted, "It won't be easy. I'm just
beginning, but I know everyone in the business."

Tina extended her hand across the old, scarred desk.
"I'm just beginning, too, and I don't know anyone."
Kay laughed and took Tina's hand. Her new client was
strong and young and determined; all she needed was
someone to believe in her dream. Kay Cooper was that
someone.

"Now for the hard part." Kay put her glasses back
on, picked up a pencil and began making notes. She

talked to Tina as she scribbled, ticking off all the things that were wrong with her new client. The list was long. "But not insurmountable," she assured Tina. "The big hurdle is weight. Once you get over that one, the rest—the makeup, clothes, hair—will be easy. But first we get rid of the baby fat. I know, I know, you've been told your weight is perfect for your height, and that's true—unless you plan to be a model. Lose ten pounds and the plump body will be a sleek body, the good cheekbones will be fabulous cheekbones, the beautiful face a work of art." Tina believed every word. Within a month she was renamed Bettina and sent out on her first rounds; in two years she was at the top.

Not one of Kay's superlatives had been wrong. Not one of her hopes had been misplaced. They climbed the ladder together. Kay, who demanded top dollar for Bettina and got it, moved her offices to a Park Avenue penthouse and began to build up a stable of high-priced models. One other person joined them on the ladder. David Stern, already a hot young photographer, cemented his reputation with his early photos of Bettina, using a long lens to find the mystery in cobalt-blue eyes that gazed from a complexion as creamy as magnolias. Her face, framed by a rich mane of auburn hair, was frozen on film by the shutters of other cameras, too, and soon Bettina's face adorned the covers of *Vogue*, *Mademoiselle*, *Bazaar* and the early issues of *W*.

Tina flipped through the pages of the album—Bettina in swim wear, designer gowns, breathy lingerie; extreme close-ups of her now famous eyes, sultry beneath lids dusted with a famous brand of eye shadow; lips smiling enigmatically, frosted with a new color gloss. Each time she was different; yet each time she projected the essence that had been created for her and by her—the sexuality, beauty, intelligence of Bettina. It was heady, her fame, and it lasted for seven more years.

Tina paused at an especially provocative tear sheet from one of her last jobs. Her hair had been wind-blown by David's electric fan and tumbled carelessly around her face; her eyes were ornately lined and her hands clasped behind her head. David's camera had framed her from just along the rise of her breasts, and she appeared to be nude. A strand of cultured pearls was caught in her red, pouting lips. That had been a first, the beginning of the sensual ads that were to get bolder and bolder over the years; but by then, Bettina would be gone.

The remaining photographs in the album were more recent: Kam and Eli on the roof of Timberline in a last-ditch effort to stop leaks with buckets of tar; Kam making pancakes; Eli at a campfire.... Tina had flipped the pages quickly, passing over their early days at Timberline. Now she paused and forced herself to turn back to the picture of Bryant taking down the For Sale sign the day they bought the inn.

Tall and thin, his blond hair in need of a trim, Bryant looked much younger than his thirty years. Her eyes moved to the next shot, the two of them on the porch. They were both smiling broadly, and Bryant had one arm firmly around his wife's shoulder. Tina studied her image closely. She'd looked like a kid then, too, grinning and ebullient. There was a glow in both their faces, an anticipation for the great adventure lying ahead that had brought them so much happiness—in the beginning.

Almost angrily, Tina slammed the book closed. She was no longer in the mood to reminisce. She slipped off her robe and slippers and crawled into bed. But the past wouldn't let go; it nagged at her mind, and she found herself waking with it during the night. When she got up at dawn, Tina felt as tired as when she'd gone to bed.

Kam was in the kitchen, making the morning's first big pot of coffee. Tina stood in the doorway and watched him at the stove. He wore a big blue apron lettered with the words *The New York City Ballet*, and his wheat-colored hair was pulled back in a band at the nape of his neck. Kammie: part intellectual, part flower child, all mountain spirit, he'd decided to live in the Rockies when he first arrived at the University of Colorado at the age of seventeen. He and Eli had turned up at the inn just when she needed them, and she often wondered if she could have managed without their help.

"I guess you heard about my phone call," Tina said as she poured herself a cup of coffee.

"Yeah. He was a super athlete."

Tina looked up frowning. "Who?"

"Adam Cole. Quarterback for the Erie Lakers the first year they joined the league. Had several good years and then got hurt. He would have been one of the great ones," Kam declared as he began setting out the pots and pans for the morning breakfast. "We need more eggs," he said. "I better go down to Boulder this afternoon."

Tina nodded as she pulled the breakfast menus from her skirt pocket and handed them to him. "Same as yesterday. We have enough eggs for breakfast, don't we?"

Kam glanced at the menu. "Easily," he answered. "Course, quarterback to cosmetics king isn't exactly your everyday transition, but he's done okay."

Tina kept ahead of his quick change of subject. "It's not Adam Cole I'm concerned about. It's me."

Kam lined a skillet with thick strips of bacon before he looked over at Tina. "Why? You're gorgeous."

"Thanks, pal. But even if it's true, that might not be good enough."

"What's the matter? Scared?"

Tina took a sip of coffee and cradled the warm cup in her hands before answering. "I don't know. Part of me feels a sense of adventure, not just for the money but to prove that I can do it. The other part, the sensible part, sends up all kinds of warning signals. I ran before, Kam. I ran away from New York and that kind of life."

Kam nodded. "Sure. I get that." He'd come from the East and understood the intimidation of big cities. "It's not for everybody. But it was your thing once, Tina. You thrived on it."

Tina smiled. "I was young. And tough."

"You're even tougher now. Hell, strength—physical and mental—is the first requirement for owning a place like this. You're strong, okay."

"But not so young."

Kam reached up and took a kitchen fork from the row of utensils above the stove. Carefully, he turned the bacon. Then he looked back at Tina. "Right now, in that denim skirt with your hair pulled back, you look about fifteen."

"But I'm almost thirty-six, and in my profession—or my ex-profession—that's over the hill."

"All in your mind," Kam said philosophically. "Besides, you're supposed to be the mother, right?"

"True, but the fashion world is a world of illusions. Everyone's young and beautiful," Tina remembered.

Kam laughed. "Well, I can't fight that kind of illogical thinking."

"Should I try it again?" she wondered aloud, thinking about the life she'd abandoned.

"Eli thinks so. I'm not sure. But it's your life, Tina, and you're going to have to decide." He smiled at her. "I figured you'd need some thinking time, so I saddled Mountain Dew. She's hobbled by the back door. Take a ride. We've got the makings of a beautiful day out there—clear and crisp." When Tina hesitated, he gave her a playful kick with the toe of his boot. "Go on. Eli can take care of the dining room."

Tina rode the mare toward town, turning off onto a trail just before she reached the settlement of Silver Hill and heading for the pass. Mountain Dew carefully picked her way along what once, a hundred years before, had been the stagecoach route. It hugged the hill on one side and dropped off on the other side to the valley a few hundred feet below. Mountain Dew knew the pace and never failed to stop at a widening in the trail, where Tina slipped off and scrambled along the hill to a rock outcropping with a breathtaking view of the divide.

"I won't be leaving all this," she said aloud, causing the little mare to prick up her ears. "I'll just be going away for a few months. *If* I go."

Not even a few months, she thought, correcting her spoken words. Probably only a few days. That's all it would take for Adam Cole to decide against her. The ex-football hero turned cosmetic tycoon probably hadn't heard of Tina Lawrence or even Bettina; or if he did know about her, he knew she'd run away, deserting a campaign not unlike the one he was getting ready to launch. She was bad insurance. Tina imagined that a lot—possibly everything—was riding on this campaign for Adam Cole. He wouldn't be about to take any chances. Even if he liked her looks.

"She's beautiful, all right," Adam said as his eyes flicked over the composite of Bettina. "A sensational-looking woman. Or she *was*," he amended. "Ten or twelve years ago."

"Keep looking," his advertising director suggested laconically. Bill Fontana had showed up at the door of Adam's office at nine o'clock sharp, knowing that his boss would be at his desk, probably had been there for more than an hour. Adam Cole was an early riser; by eight o'clock he'd run his four-mile course along the East River, showered, dressed, eaten a light breakfast and walked the twenty blocks from his apartment to his office.

Bill liked to get to him first thing in the morning before the rush of secretaries and assistants began to monopolize his time. If he didn't beat the morning rush, he usually waited until evening, sometimes calling Adam at home or arranging a meeting in a neighborhood bar. Early morning, late night; Bill knew his boss would be sharp at either time. Adam Cole saw midnight pass and dawn rise every day of his life. He didn't have time for long hours of sleep.

"Kay Cooper sent the photos over," Bill told his boss. "She was struck by the amazing resemblance."

He sat back, giving Adam time to sift through the stack of photos until he got to the most recent ones.

Adam stopped occasionally, pausing to scrutinize Tina's face as Bill watched silently. Finally Adam leaned back and loosened his tie. His shirt sleeves were already rolled halfway up his smooth muscular arms. Although he'd been out of professional sports for years, at thirty-eight he still had the lean, hard body of an athlete and made sure his shirts were tailored to fit perfectly across his broad shoulders and taper to his slim waist. He picked up one of the pictures. "You're right, of course. The resemblance between them is remarkable." On the other end of his desk were the latest photographs of his daughter, Holly. His eyes, unreadable, flicked toward them and then back to Bettina.

"This is a million-dollar campaign," Bill reminded his boss, "and we've got to have the best to pull it off."

"No one knows that better than I do, friend," Adam answered.

"Well, she used to be the best." Bill lowered his six-foot-six frame into a chair opposite Adam's desk while Adam continued to study a photo of Bettina in a simple long white dress; she was staring coolly ahead in a classic pose that seemed totally natural.

"This one's probably nine or ten years ago, right?" Adam was still wary.

Bill shrugged. "So's the last one in the stack. Take a look at it."

Adam looked down at the remaining picture, the jewelry ad with the pearls clutched provocatively between her teeth.

"Good Lord. That was a little before its time, huh?"

Bill nodded. "She started something there—she and Stern."

"Why did she quit, Bill?"

Bill shrugged again. "I don't know. Just blew town when she was right at the top. Took off for Wyoming or Arizona or one of those places." Bill, born and reared in Montclair, New Jersey, thought anything west of Pittsburgh was foreign territory.

"Why?" Adam prodded. "Drugs? Alcohol?"

"Not that I've heard. Seems like she just got tired of the life. I do know Fred Carlson hasn't recovered yet."

Adam looked up, a frown creasing his forehead.

"Bettina was all set for his first major campaign when she bailed," Bill reminded.

"Great," came the sarcastic reply. "I should have known it was something like that." Adam pushed the pictures aside and stood up. He began to move around the office restlessly, pacing up and down in front of the large windows, ignoring the panoramic view of New York. Physical activity was an outlet for him, especially when he was either angry or worried. Bill suspected the latter now.

"Like you said, Bill, this is a make-or-break campaign. Everything's riding on it. We can't afford to hire a model who left the business almost ten years ago under questionable circumstances—particularly if there's a chance she'd give a repeat performance."

"I couldn't agree more," Bill said as he unfolded himself from the chair and gathered up the photographs. "But we haven't hired her, Adam. I just want to have a look, and I'm sure you do, too. The resemblance to Holly is uncanny, certainly worth a test."

Bill, having achieved his purpose, found time to express a few doubts of his own. "Maybe she really doesn't resemble Holly. Maybe she no longer photographs like a lily." He shuffled the photos, putting the last one—the pearls ad—on top and letting out a low whistle before continuing to list his doubts. "Maybe she's fat and ugly..." He started for the door, photos in hand, and then turned back to look at Adam. "Or maybe she's everything you've ever dreamed of."

Adam's dark eyes were thoughtful. "Test her, Bill. Let's find out."

Chapter 2

They barreled down the mountain in the old brown Timberline van, Kam driving, Tina holding on for dear life.

"I have hours before my flight leaves, Kam; we don't have to break any records."

"It's no fun if I don't break a record," Kam replied, sending gravel flying as he headed into a curve. The road from Timberline to the small town of Silver Hill was unpaved and hung precariously over the side of the mountain with no guardrails. "No one's ever gone off this mountain," Kam declared, "even in a snowstorm."

"That's because Coloradians have a certain respect for the wildness of their surroundings. But let's try to keep their record intact," she added, grasping the armrest. "I'm nervous enough as it is."

Obediently, Kam slowed down and when they reached the highway managed to travel at a reasonable speed through Boulder and across the plains toward the Denver airport. "So you're worried about your decision," he observed finally.

"No, just overly excited." She *was* worried, very worried, but she tried to hide her trepidation under a mask of excitement. "Adam Cole likes the idea," she said for perhaps the tenth time that day, to convince herself as well as Kam. "He was intrigued by the resemblance between his daughter and me, or so Kay says. He thinks the combination might be just what his campaign needs. Of course, he wants test shots," she assured Kam and—once more—herself. "No one would mount a campaign like this without tests."

Kam nodded his head in agreement and waited for Tina to continue working her way through the now-familiar scenario that she'd played out again and again since she'd returned from her morning ride that day last week, her decision made.

"And if it doesn't work out," Tina went on, "and I'm certainly not counting on it—well, I still have the inn."

"You'll always have the inn—and Eli and me to help take care of it."

"I know that, Kam, but if I could get this job— think of the difference it would make. Think of what we'd be able to do. Think of the improvements! With a central-heating system that was dependable, we'd get the winter guests back year after year instead of losing them along the way."

"Yeah," Kam agreed. "Every time there're a few days with no heat, we lose all the weaklings."

Tina laughed. "Unfortunately, everyone doesn't have your constitution."

"Well, a warm place would make a lot of difference. So would a gourmet kitchen. If we could expand the menu, maybe get a real chef..."

"Quit counting pennies at the grocery store..."

"Stock the lake with fish..." Kam began to fantasize along with Tina.

"Buy a new wagon and more tents for the overnight camping trips..."

"Cut new trails and fix up the stables..."

They were both getting into it now, gleefully thinking about the future of Timberline. "*If* I get the job," Tina said finally, her giggles ended.

"You'll get it," Kam assured her.

Two hours later, after more words of assurance and a final hug, Kam left her at the airport, and Tina was on her way, returning to a city from which she'd fled nine years earlier with the vow never to return.

Never say never, Tina, she mentally chided herself as she buckled her seat belt. There was no turning back now, and there was no avoiding the memories that came rushing toward her at a speed equal to the plane's propulsion toward New York. The years whisked by, one image replacing another too quickly to comprehend. Mentally, she tried to reach out and stop the rush of years, but her memory refused to pause until that last year when Bettina herself had stopped, looked around and realized that she was almost at the end of her rope.

At twenty-six, she'd been exhausted—and frightened. She'd learned during her struggle to reach the top and stay there that fame had a dark underside, and it was vanity. After a career of looking over her shoulder, fearful of aging in a profession where youth dictated success, Tina had begun to wonder who she was, how she felt and what she thought. None of that had mattered before; nothing had mattered except how she looked. Suddenly she was tired of trying to look eighteen, even more tired of pretending that she cared.

Kay had known how she felt; so had her press agent, her accountant, the makeup man who worked with her full-time, her hairdresser and all of the photographers, especially David. All her entourage had known that Bettina was at the edge, but none of them had admitted it. She was too valuable a commodity to lose.

Tina had become an image frozen by the camera for the world to scrutinize, and she'd worked harder and harder to maintain that image with no clue to her own identity. She'd rushed from one assignment to the next, always under pressure to look fresh and youthful, and she hadn't had a vacation in years because she'd been afraid that if she once got off the merry-go-round called fame, she'd never be able to climb back on again. She was an image; that's all there was to Bettina. But there was more to Tina Lawrence; there had to be.

Bryant had been the first one to understand how she felt. She'd opened up to him, telling him her innermost doubts and fears, telling him what she'd only intimated to the others. Bryant was an illustrator, and a good one, according to David, who had very slyly invited them both to one of his studio parties for a hundred or more friends, knowing that even in the crowd, those two would find each other. But just in case, he'd made a point of introducing them early in the evening.

"I believe Bettina could use a breath of fresh air about now," he'd said, with a meaning that went be-

yond the crowded party. For the first time Tina had
realized that David not only knew but cared about
what she was going through.

There had been something magical about Bryant, a
tall, thin young man with serious blue eyes that
seemed to look right into her heart. It had happened
so quickly, barely before they'd spoken more than a
few words. He *knew* her, and she felt good with him.
She hadn't felt good with anyone—especially herself—in a long, long time. He was quiet, gentle and
thoughtful, and Tina fell in love with him almost at
once.

Tina was never sure whose idea it was—hers or
Bryant's—to flee New York and buy the old Colorado inn. It was probably mutual and had come out of
a simultaneous desire to be rid of the city. They'd begun to think as one. Bryant hated city life as much as
Tina, hated the surface glamour that didn't quite cover
what was vain and often sordid beneath.

Once the decision had been made, they'd moved
quickly. They made plans to use Tina's money, a large
part of her savings, for the down payment and the
early renovations on Timberline Inn while all the time
Kay was voicing her opposition loudly and firmly.

"You're crazy," she'd said bluntly. "Neither of you
knows the first thing about running a hotel in the
mountains."

"What's to know?" Tina had asked breezily. "We
can always hire someone to help out."

"But—but—" Kay hadn't even been able to find
the words for her perplexity. She might have grown up
in the South, but as far as she was concerned, everything of importance began and ended in New York,

especially for a model of Bettina's status. "What the hell will you do there?" she'd finally managed to ask.

"We'll *live*, Kay. We'll run the inn. Bryant will paint, and I'll have babies."

Kay had rolled her eyes heavenward. "If you do insist on getting married and having a family, you could take a leave of absence. Babies are born in New York every day, so I'm told." Then she'd voiced her real concern. "A sabbatical of some sort would be acceptable, but if you just leave, walk away, your reputation will be ruined. Listen to me, honey, you've got commitments. There're all sorts of deals in the works, and the Carlson contract alone is worth thousands to you."

"Fred Carlson can find someone else to model his coats, Kay. You can find someone."

"But he wants Bettina."

Tina had shaken her head. "I'm not Bettina anymore, remember? I'm Tina Lawrence, and very soon I'll be Mrs. Bryant Harris of Timberline Inn, Colorado."

Kay had let escape a moan of disapproval. "That's not about your marriage," she'd assured Tina when the moan had ended. "I think it's wonderful that you and Bryant made that decision. He's a lovely person, and so are you. I'm sure you'll be very happy—if you stay in New York."

"No, Kay," Tina had answered firmly, not willing to go into it any further. The decision had been made. They'd already submitted a bid on the property. They were on their way.

Kay had tried one more tack. "All of this is very unprofessional, and when the Carlson story gets out, no one—I mean absolutely no one—will take a chance on you again.''

"I don't care, Kay," Tina had said emphatically. "I'm not planning to come back."

"Well, someday you'll change your mind about that. Someday you'll be ready to come back, and they'll all remember what happened. Walking out like this makes you look like you're . . . you're . . ."

"Crazy?" Tina had laughed out loud. "Well, if this is craziness, I want more of it. I've never been so happy. Please don't spoil it for me with lectures, Kay. There'll be other models a hundred times more beautiful than Bettina to fill these jobs, but I only have one life, and I want to live it with Bryant. Be happy for us."

Defeated but still doubting, Kay had complied by grabbing Tina in a bear hug. There was no arguing against a plea that had so touched her heart.

Tina had taken a little residual guilt with her to Colorado. She was haunted by the fact that she hadn't handled the Carlson contract more gracefully. He wasn't a forgiving kind of man, and the lies that he'd probably spread about her hasty exodus began to haunt Tina. When the lies actually reached her, Tina longed to refute them, but Bryant dissuaded her.

"Forget it, babe. We have enough to do here without worrying about Carlson. He's old history. So is New York. We've got *now*—and we're going to grab on to it and have a good ride."

So she tried not to listen as the rumors kept floating back to her in letters from friends outside the business—that she was being labeled a quitter or at least a coward and possibly mentally unbalanced. Other stories—started by Carlson, according to the scuttlebutt—told of the once beautiful Bettina now grossly overweight or of her face scarred in an accident. No one in that bright and glittering world that she had left behind could believe she'd had the nerve just to walk away.

Soon the rumors stopped, or another scandal replaced the disgrace of Bettina, or possibly her friends—and her enemies—found other topics to occupy their time. Eventually she stopped hearing from anyone except Kay and, occasionally, David. Kay's phone calls came once or twice a month, and David sent her long talky tapes whenever he had time.

The inn became their passion, all consuming, devouring money, demanding time and never really paying for itself, but there were compensations. Bryant's paintings began to catch on. Galleries in the resorts of Vail, Aspen and Steamboat Springs hung his work, and he slowly began to build up a following. Tina insisted that Bryant set aside more time to work in his studio, even though this meant longer hours for her. She didn't complain, and if either of them ever regretted their sudden move, they never mentioned it. The mountains were in turn beautiful and serene, wild and fierce, but always, always, this was home. They never looked back.

There was only one sadness. The hoped-for baby didn't arrive, and after five years of marriage Tina and Bryant began to realize that part of their dream might never come true. However, they were optimistic about adoption, and when they made their first appointment at a Denver agency, Tina's dream of motherhood blossomed again.

Then her world shattered around her—so quickly and with such finality that it took months for Tina to comprehend the magnitude of her loss. With the profits from his paintings, Bryant had made a down payment on a small plane to fly guests from Denver to an airfield in the valley just ten miles below Timberline and to shuttle passengers—and his canvases—to the ski country. It was an extravagant purchase, but with luck Bryant felt it could turn a profit and help put Timberline in the black. Across the fuselage of the plane, he'd painted the *Timberline* logo that represented the inn and his art studio. He was on a flight alone to the gallery in Vail when the plane went down. It was a calm January night with no storm in sight, clear and starlit. The *Timberline* suddenly lost altitude, crashed into the mountain and burst into flame. No reason for the accident was ever discovered.

Stubbornly and against all advice, Tina vowed to stay in Colorado to continue what she and Bryant had begun. Timberline had been their dream together, and she wasn't going to abandon it. Not ever. But without the additional income from the sale of Bryant's paintings, the going became more difficult each year, and it wasn't long before his insurance was gulped up by necessary repairs, mortgages and taxes. She couldn't handle it alone, and when Kam and Eli turned up—literally on her doorstep—Tina took them in. The old Timberline van became the commuter, supply and grocery bus. Fortunately, Kam was able to keep it running. But the dream of Timberline that had been so close grew fainter and fainter with each new, difficult season. To keep it a reality, she'd finally given in to Kay's urgings.

The memory of Bryant and what they'd built together brought her full circle... back to New York.

"A limo! Kay, this is—" Tina struggled for the proper superlative.

"No more than you deserve," Kay said briskly, grabbing Tina's arm and shepherding her into the limousine. "I wanted you to return in style, not like country-come-to-town."

"Even if that's exactly what I am," Tina admitted.

"Not you, honey," Kay countered. "Never you." As the driver pulled out of the bottleneck of La Guardia traffic, Kay settled comfortably into the plush leather seat and smiled. "At last," she said, "you're back."

"And except for you, I doubt if any heads are turning."

"You'd be surprised. David Stern is beside himself. He's doing your tests." Kay paused for Tina's sigh of relief. "I figured that we might as well stack the deck in our favor as much as possible. With Adam Cole pushing us to get the shots done right away... He wanted to see you at the studio today; can you imagine?" Kay narrowed her blue eyes and looked at Tina critically, not as a friend this time but as an agent, searching out imperfections, no matter how small.

Tina, used to such inspection from Kay over the years, smiled. "A good night's sleep wouldn't hurt, huh?"

"You said it, honey. I'm going to take you to my place and put you right to bed. And then—"

"You don't have to tell me. I need to lose five pounds—if I get the job."

"You'll get it; you'll get it," Kay assured her. "And the magic number is ten. Ten pounds, honey, and I'm relieved to see that we don't have too many other problems. I was afraid the struggle with that damned inn would show somehow—in your skin tone or dark circles or lines around the mouth—"

"Look closer, Kay. They're all there."

"Not so you'd notice," Kay said encouragingly. "Besides, you're a *mother* this time, for God's sake. They can't expect you to be flawless."

"Yes, they can," Tina countered with a laugh. "But I'm glad to be back; at least it means seeing you again." Tina sighed. "A lot has happened since then, hasn't it?"

Kay felt the tears well up in her eyes and blinked quickly to avoid Tina's seeing too much sentimentality under her usual optimistic exterior. "And the best is yet to be," she assured her friend.

"Well, you haven't changed," Tina offered. Kay's unceasing optimism, her determination to see only the positives in life, had always been, for Tina, both a cause of irritation and a constant source of hope.

"Lord, I wish that were true." Kay ran her fingers through her short sandy hair. "A few more gray hairs have been added to the basic dishwater blond—due to my more difficult clients. And a few more pounds added to the originally large frame—due to my husband's cooking. I'm just lucky that he's away so much. Otherwise I'd be over two hundred pounds."

Kay was exaggerating about her size. She was tall and big boned, but she carried her weight well, dressing in bulky layered outfits that created a dramatic impression. She wore with aplomb the browns and blacks and beiges that bespoke the city where she was so much at home and put them together in combinations that only an eye like Kay's could create, draping belts and scarves and shawls around and over the layers. Kay's husband was a Belgian diplomat attached to the United Nations; he was in New York perhaps one month out of two. Neither of them devoted as much time to their marriage as to their careers, and yet when they were together, they functioned beautifully as a pair. Except when she saw them socially Tina never thought of Kay as being married. Kay's life was in the business.

As their limousine approached the tunnel beneath the East River, Tina drew a deep and trembling breath of anticipation. They were almost there. Manhattan—that extraordinary island she'd left years before—was now only minutes away. Kay heard the sharp intake of breath and read the look of trepidation on Tina's face. "Butterflies?" she asked.

Tina nodded. "They're doing a fandango in my solar plexus." For the first time since her plane landed, she was giving in to her nerves...and to her fears, which revolved around one man. "Have you met him? What's he like?"

Kay knew whom she was talking about. "Yes, I've met Adam Cole, although I hardly *know* him, apart from what I hear, of course. And I hear plenty. Now, his advertising manager, Bill Fontana, is another matter. Personable, easy to communicate with—and very high on Bettina."

Tina looked out the window as they approached the toll booth. "What about Adam Cole—is he high on Bettina?" The advertising manager's recommendations carried some weight, but Tina knew as well as Kay that the final decision would be made by one man and one man alone. Adam Cole would choose his Generations Woman.

Kay knew what was going on in Tina's mind; she could see the tenseness in the way Tina held her long, lithe frame. She'd stepped off the plane uptight even though she'd hidden it well, and she'd remain uptight until she got under the lights with David's camera focused on her. Then the old magic would happen, and Tina would become Bettina. Until that moment Kay was determined not to let the tenseness turn to depression. She took her usual cheerful tack. "Adam Cole obviously knows what's best for Generations. After all, the product is his brainchild. He invested megabucks developing it, and he'll spend even more on advertising and promotion. Once he sees you and Holly together—*voilà*. He won't be able to say no."

Tina looked out the window at the stream of lights that reflected eerily around the cavernous tunnel. "Even if he's inclined to?" Tina felt sure that was the case.

"Even then," Kay determined.

"What about Holly?" Before Kay could respond, Tina began to laugh. "Nervous laughter," she reminded Kay. "I can't believe I'm sitting here asking all these questions, but I've been out of touch for so long I feel like a foreigner to all of this..." She made a sweep with her hand to encompass New York, the modeling work and the Cole family.

"Don't worry. By the time we get to my place you'll know everything I know—which, where Holly is concerned, is mostly hearsay. She's a knockout, of course, and she works a lot. Plenty of covers for teen magazines, but she's also one of the youngest girls to make the cover of a major fashion magazine. You'll recognize that face the minute you see it. Gorgeous."

"So's her father, I understand."

"Oh, yes, you'll also recognize him. He hasn't had any *Vogue* covers, but he's in almost every magazine's gossip column."

"I'm afraid I haven't been keeping up with the jet set," Tina said.

"I detect a little note of pride there."

Tina laughed, less nervously than before. "You're right; I never missed the social whirl, but I guess I better get used to it quick."

"Damned right," Kay said. "Don't let on for a minute that you're bored with all the fa-la-la. At least, not until after you get the job." Then she added, "Both the Coles, father and daughter, are a bit flamboyant, and I expect he's going to want his Generations Woman to have some of the same style. Just because you're cast as a mother, don't expect him to go for a 'matron.' Anyway, you'll find the old spark to satisfy him," Kay assured her. "I don't have any idea where the real Adam Cole ends and the image begins, but I think we can work with him."

"Well, fill me in on everything you know—the real and the fake—so I can go in armed."

Kay could tell that Tina was getting into the spirit. In the old days, she'd always researched her clients and learned their likes and dislikes, making an attempt to understand a little about the people she worked for. That was one of her assets, the intellectual approach that topped off the beauty.

"He's very competitive, obviously." Kay began her rundown on the man who held Tina's future in his hands. "He likes to win, and he loves winners. I believe that's why Holly works so hard." Knowing Tina was confused by that, Kay elaborated. "All that hard work—long hours and the extracurricular activities that Adam Cole was famous for from just about the time he left football—didn't sit so well with his wife, apparently. They say that she wanted him to bring in the wealth without going to the office, so to speak. When she left, walking out on both of them, Holly went right to work like her father. I mean it; she couldn't have been more than twelve, but the kid decided to be a model. Used to show up at sessions with a nurse, a tutor and God knows who else, a whole retinue. She's been working ever since. I always assumed she did it to please Adam. I hear she adores him. She looked around at the tender age of twelve, saw that her mother was a little lazy but liked money and that her father was a workaholic who craved success. She opted to go her father's route; since he was all she had, there really wasn't much choice. But what a quick way to grow up. She's not even sixteen yet, and she's been working a heavy schedule for four years." Kay shook her head. "Of course, she's terribly successful, and why not?" Kay sighed. "Five foot ten, one hundred and fifteen pounds—an agent's dream. Oh, if only she were mine!"

"And her mother?"

"Who knows? Pam lives abroad, I think. The divorce was very bitter. With Adam it seems to be all or nothing. He fought Pam for custody and got it. I'm sure he's fond of the girl, but he's also fond of winning. Success. And you can be sure he'll do everything in his power to make Generations the biggest success yet."

"With all that work, I wonder how he has time for the activities that put him on the society page," Tina mused aloud.

"They say the man never sleeps," was Kay's response. "And in spite of all the women he's gone out with, apparently there's been no one for him, really, since Pam. She was stunning, so I hear. Never saw her myself..." Kay, having exhausted the subject, was quiet as the limo emerged from the tunnel and headed across town.

Tina blinked at the sudden brightness of the sun that assaulted her along with the noise. She'd hoped to tiptoe back into Manhattan tentatively and quietly, alone in a cab, but she found herself plunging right into the heart of the city in a speeding limousine. She could hear the sounds of New York well enough, even in the closed car, but she could also feel it, feel the beat and pulse of the city surging through her. Traffic rushed forward and then screeched to a halt and finally inched along the avenue; buses groaned as they released their passengers; pedestrians surged into the streets oblivious to the cacophony of horns. On a street corner a tall black man sold salted pretzels from a wagon, and in a patch of bright green park workers on a lunch break from their offices turned eager faces to the autumn sun. Tina felt a brief rush of tears to her eyes; she was back, and the excitement of New York hit her as it had that first day seventeen years before.

Kay watched Tina as she stared avidly out the window with blue eyes drinking in the sights of the city as a desert absorbs a much-needed rain, and the agent smiled before settling back happily, assured that everything was going to be all right.

The next morning Kay still held on to that optimism, even though she did so with some difficulty. Tina arrived at David's studio with her just-shampooed hair hanging damply to her shoulders, no makeup, ready to turn herself over to David's band of assistants, and she was a bundle of nerves.

"You look wonderful," Kay assured her, and it was true. No one had the natural beauty, scrubbed clean and without a trace of powder or paint, of Bettina. But the nerves were another matter. Kay was beginning to wonder, for the first time, if Tina could carry it off. Nine years was a long time to be away from the cameras.

David gave her a warm hug and a kiss, looked at her carefully and nodded his approval before turning her over to makeup. "Don't worry," he assured Kay sotto voce as Tina sat stiffly in a chair across the room while her hair was set on giant hot rollers and the makeup artists went to work on her face. "She'll be as good as ever."

David had changed more than any of them, his once lean silhouette now generously padded with forty extra pounds, but his manner was the same. David Stern was the only photographer Tina had ever worked with who never raised his voice, never rushed around giving orders and acting generally hysterical. He was calm and orderly, always knowing exactly what he wanted. His staff understood that and complied with his commands, spoken quickly, occasionally with sarcasm but never with anger.

At last Tina was ready for his inspection. He led her to the no-seam paper that was all the background he wanted for Bettina's test and studied her as carefully as Kay had earlier.

"Well?" Tina asked at last. Her throat was dry, and the word cracked.

"Get Bettina a glass of water," David said quietly, and like a shot, the water was there. Tina gulped it down and tried again. "Well?"

"Well, some of the innocence has gone, but I like what's replaced it. Yes, you'll do," he said, repeating the words he'd spoken to her all those years ago, and Tina felt herself begin—just begin—to relax.

"Time?" David asked no one in particular.

"Eight-thirty," came the answer.

"Well, King Cole and his entourage are late, and since I have another session at eleven, we'll need to get started without them. I can't wait all day even if Century's paying the bills."

Tina shot a worried look toward Kay, who ignored it, or tried to, hiding her own anxiety. Kay wasn't thrilled that Adam Cole was a half hour late, and as she returned the bright reassuring smile to Tina, she prayed silently that she hadn't brought her friend all the way from Colorado for a disappointment. If he didn't show at all it wouldn't be the first time that a corporation head, after listening to the advice of his advertising department, had okayed a shoot and then decided against it, for whatever whim, with no explanations to anyone. Kay had been in the business long enough to know that while her girls couldn't miss a session for anything short of death, the same rules didn't seem to apply in reverse.

"Come on, Bettina," David urged. "Let's get to work." He looked over at her once more, critically. "God, I hate that dress, but it's what was sent over. It's not you at all."

Tina agreed. The dress, far too frilly and young for her, was also too small. It clung to her figure and, she feared, rather than looking sexy, gave her the appearance of a dowdy matron trying to imitate a young model.

Yet when she began to work, all her sharp pangs of nerves and the drifting, shifting anxiety that had gripped her since she made the decision to return to New York disappeared. There was nothing but the lights, the rock music blaring from a tape deck in the background, the click of the ubiquitous camera—and David's voice.

"Wonderful, darling. Look at me. Now turn, just a fraction. That's it. Great. Once more. Now lower your head. Yes, yes. Perfect." David's voice was there, cajoling, caressing, applauding, teasing, commanding, and she obeyed that voice as she always had, losing herself in the movement and the moment.

David stepped around her, as gracefully as ever despite his added weight, shooting from every angle. When he reached the end of a roll, he pulled the camera from around his neck, held out his hand for a replacement and started shooting again while an assistant reloaded. Every move was made without a pause, without a hitch. Leaning over David's shoulder, a second assistant changed camera settings as the shutter clicked away, bracketing the exposure on each shot to cover changes and nuances in the lighting. Everything came back to Tina as she worked, all of David's idiosyncrasies, and as she remembered, she felt like Bettina again.

Finally, David sat back on his heels, satisfied. "Okay, that's it," he said, and around the room, one by one, the lights were switched off. "That was good."

"Yes, it was very good indeed," a man's voice agreed from the shadows. The voice was low and husky yet tinged with authority, and as Tina shaded her eyes with her hand and tried to peer beyond the one remaining floodlight, it, too, shut off and she saw him.

He was better looking than she'd expected; his photographs hadn't done justice to the crisp texture of his dark hair or the depth of his brown eyes. He wore a silk shirt and a six-hundred-dollar suit that was tailored perfectly to his hard, taut body. Tina hadn't the slightest doubt that she was in the presence of the man in charge.

Kay materialized beside him with a wide smile.

"Bring her over, Kay," Adam said, not quite reflecting her smile.

"Tina, honey," Kay responded, "come and meet Adam Cole."

Tina moved forward, feeling suddenly awkward, too big and too old for the dress she wore. The strangeness of this world she'd just reentered suddenly seemed unnatural to her again, as unnatural as the costume she wore. She stood before him barefoot and not at all the woman she wished to project—the Generations Woman. She could see in his eyes that she wasn't what he had expected.

"Glad to meet you, Miss Lawrence. I'm pleased you could fly in for the test." His tone underlined the final word as he took her hand in his strong grasp. When Tina looked up into his face, she saw the constraint written there, and she knew that he was going to have to be convinced.

He looked away after a long moment and nodded at David. "Glad you got started without us." No apology, no explanation for his lateness was forthcoming. "Where'd you get the dress?" he asked David.

"Your people sent it over."

"Hmm," was the noncommital response to that news. "Why's her hair up?"

"The sketches show it up." David couldn't be intimidated. "But I'm planning to shoot a roll with it down."

"Yes, I think that's a good idea." He answered David but looked at Tina intently. "How do you usually wear it?"

Tina lifted her hand to touch her hair, which had been swept back from her face and wrapped loosely around her head. "Most of the time I . . ."

"Wear it down, I think." Unexpectedly, he leaned forward and pulled the pins from her heavy hair. Tina tried to step away, but his hands held her. He removed each pin, slowly, deliberately, and then said, "Yes, that's much better." His hands were warm on her face but commanding. Then he spoke again, and his words belied the touch. They might have been directed to makeup or wardrobe or to his own advertising department, but they were spoken to her. "I want a woman exulting in her maturity," he said, "not someone who looks like she's off the farm."

Face flaming, Tina moved away. There had been momentary excitement in the quickening of her breath, the pounding of her heart when Adam touched her. Now there was only anger—at his arrogance, at his assumption that he knew what was best for her and at his blatant attempt to establish domination, not just over the shooting and everyone involved with it but over Tina—and in front of a studio filled with people.

Tina's eyes flashed dangerously, and Kay must have seen that a confrontation that could ruin everything was in the air. She stepped forward quickly. "Tina's hair is glorious; it *should* hang free," she agreed. "And when you see her beside your daughter...where is Holly?" she asked in an effort to swing the conversation around and stop whatever was happening between Tina and Adam.

Adam wasn't unaware of Kay's motives, but he just shrugged. "She'll be here soon." As he spoke a voice could be heard from the outer office.

"Why do I have to test when I have the job already?"

The answer of the man who followed behind her was lost as Holly Cole swept into the studio. Kay had been right, Tina thought; she recognized the girl immediately—tall and elegant and terribly beautiful in spite of the definitely unhappy look around her mouth and the huge round sunglasses that hid her eyes.

The man behind Holly finally caught up, passed her and rushed over to greet Tina. "I'm Bill Fontana," he said, "and a big fan of yours. This is Holly Cole." He gave Holly a nudge forward.

But the girl was balking. She ignored Tina's smile of welcome but didn't miss Tina's outfit. "No way, Bill, am I going to pose in something like that—not even for your wonderful Generations line. Besides, I'm tired of all these mother types you keep finding for me to pose with. Why can't you hire a stand-in for me? It's getting boring."

"Holly." Adam's voice was low and controlled with a hard edge of anger beneath.

Holly's struggle showed on her face. She wanted to cause a scene and show her anger at being in the studio against her will, and yet her father's look and tone brooked no further displays of temperament. "All right," she said, whipping off her glasses to reveal blue eyes more enormous and beautiful than Tina had remembered from photographs. "But let's be quick with it."

"My sentiments exactly," David responded. Throughout the whole scene, he'd been sitting on his stool, camera strung around his neck waiting. "No time for prima donnas today, Holly. I'm behind schedule as it is." He got down from the stool and motioned to Tina and Holly. "Let's see you together."

With a shrug of acquiescence, Holly moved into position. Her outfit of hot-pink tights, ankle-high boots and a bulky striped sweater that reached almost to her knees wasn't quite appropriate for the shooting. In fact, she looked like some rare exotic creature temporarily on display under the glare of bright searching lights—a creature that might make her escape at any minute. Tina looked at her out of the corner of her eye, cautiously, to avoid any further comment. It was going to be quite a job, she judged, to mother this one—even on film.

"It's not going to work," Holly announced loudly to David, "the two of us standing side by side. I'm a good three inches taller," she declared with obvious condescension.

"Barely two inches," David corrected her. "I happen to know your exact heights. I was photographing Bettina before you were born, dear, and I started with you when you were still wearing that dreadful retainer in your mouth. This isn't a lineup, Holly, it's a photo session. Sit," he said quietly but firmly, pushing a stool toward Holly, who quickly complied. "That's a girl," he said. "Now let's get on with it."

To Holly's credit she managed to murmur a little "I'm sorry," and look contrite. Tina wondered how much was genuine. So far the girl hadn't addressed a word to her, either because she felt threatened or, more likely, because Tina wasn't worth the trouble.

Tina's thoughts were lost in another bustle of activity as David began to set up and light the shot. She tried to let his voice comfort her as the orders began. "I think I'll start close in for the head shots, so give me a 1O5 lens. Keep the pink gel, and let's try a bounce board. Tina, stand a little behind. That's it. Bring your shoulder forward. Fine. Somebody do something about Holly's nose—it's shining. Powder her down. Okay. That's good." Within a matter of seconds, each of those commands had been obeyed, and David was ready.

During the next hour as they worked, Tina felt none of the excitement of the earlier session, when she'd been alone with David. She was stiff, frozen, as if her smile was pasted on. David worked with her easily, spoke to her just as before, but nothing could bring her up to the vibrancy of the girl. Beside Holly, Tina felt awkward—and old. Doubles—posing with another model—had always been tough for Tina; today was worse than ever.

Her feelings of discomfort weren't helped by the fact that Adam Cole was there, somewhere in the shadows, watching her, judging her, deciding if she was good enough, if she still had it. Tina cursed silently to herself, wishing she'd never agreed to do the shoot, wishing she were home in Colorado.

Changing positions with Holly at last, Tina sat on the stool and hoped to relax. But she still longed for home or, lacking that, an escape to Kay's and a hot

bath to make her forget New York, this studio and
Adam Cole.

But she couldn't forget him because he was the reason she had come back. In his decision was power, the
power to save Timberline. She tried to keep that
thought uppermost in her mind as, drained and exhausted, she listened to David and tried to respond to
his commands. Why, she wondered, didn't David realize what was happening? Couldn't he see her tenseness through his lens? Was he losing his touch? The
thoughts ran through Tina's head until, at last, it was
over.

Adam emerged from the background and walked
toward her. He'd loosened his tie, revealing the strong
cording of his neck and the gleam of a gold chain
against his skin. Tina had forgotten that under the facade of the smooth businessman was a big spender for
whom silk and gold were among life's necessities.
She'd also forgotten that the man had once been an
athlete. His past was apparent in the carriage of his
body, the strength of his arms and shoulders, the grace
of his walk. He stopped a few feet away and smiled at
her, but his eyes revealed nothing beyond quizzical
interest. Tina had no idea whether or not Adam Cole
was pleased with what he'd seen. There was certainly
no hint that the job was hers.

"Thank you again, Miss Lawrence, for flying in.
We'll be in touch."

"Yes." Tina met his eyes evenly. She might feel ill
at ease, but she'd be damned if he was going to intim-
idate her. Adam Cole represented all that she'd fled
from—the slick facade, the empty promises, the love
of power and total ambition. Those traits belonged
here on the New York high wire; they were no longer

a part of her life. Yet if she had to play the game for a while, she'd play.

"I'll expect to be hearing from you." She smiled a smile that was pure Bettina and showed nothing of what she was thinking.

"Well, I'd better call and reserve my return ticket," Tina said later as their cab crept by millimeters through the noon traffic on its way to Kay's apartment.

"Don't be ridiculous," Kay answered. Her smile was wide and looked quite believable; still, Tina couldn't believe it for a moment.

"I didn't get it, Kay. Holly Cole made her feelings about me very obvious; I froze in my session with her, and as for her father—well, he didn't like me at all."

"Oh, I disagree, honey," Kay said, "Holly's opinion isn't going to make a bit of difference. As for the shooting, let's trust David. He's never failed us before. And about Adam," she added with a smile, "I think he liked you very much. That sexy little byplay with your hair—"

"I don't want to be his latest girlfriend," Tina interjected. "I want to work for him—I think."

"You want to work for him—you know," Kay answered. "But it's out of our hands now, so let's have a little fun this weekend. We'll hear from Century Cosmetics on Monday. In the meantime, it's all up to Adam Cole."

Chapter 3

The view from Kay's French windows downtown across Central Park was one of the best in New York, she assured Tina. However, every time Tina looked out she found herself searching the skyline for the Century Cosmetics building and trying to imagine what was going on inside its walls.

"Even Superman couldn't see it from here with his X-ray vision," Kay assured her after Tina finally admitted that she wasn't just admiring the view. "It's too far west. Besides, he's not there today; it's Saturday, remember? Or do days of the week mean nothing to you mountain people?"

Tina managed a laugh. "I thought he was a work-aholic."

"True. But he probably takes the work home. And I don't know where he lives," she hastened to add, "so come away from the window. It's a beautiful day, and we're going to have lunch at the Tavern on the Green."

"Kay, I can't afford an expensive lunch—"

"It's on me, honey. We're going to have fun this weekend and forget Adam Cole. We'll start worrying first thing Monday morning, when David sends the pictures over to his office."

Monday dawned clear and warm, even better than the weekend, a perfect fall day in New York. David Stern got to his studio early and went right to the darkroom, where he'd developed Tina's pictures late Friday night. He'd looked at each enlargement as it came from the bath, pinned it up and not looked at it again, deciding to wait until he was fresher and more objective.

Now as he went into the darkroom, flicked on the light and looked again, David realized that he hadn't changed his mind. He walked around the room pulling down the eight-by-tens, seemingly at random but with a quickly critical eye. Then he called out to his secretary, who came running, gave her the stack of pictures and the order, "Get someone to mount these and send them by messenger this morning—to Bill Fontana at Century."

Adam Cole couldn't read Bill Fontana's expression an hour later when he walked into his boss's office. "You're not going to believe these," he said, striding unannounced through the door. Bill's voice was deliberately even and noncommital.

Adam looked up from his desk, remembering the photo session with Tina. He hadn't thought of her since—not consciously, at least. An image had crept into his mind's eye once or twice during the weekend, but he'd managed to ignore it. Now the image was back, and he realized it never had disappeared completely. "That bad, eh?" he asked, aware that for a moment he felt a pang of regret.

Bill's long lean face broke into a lopsided grin. "Don't judge by what you saw at the shooting. She didn't look that vibrant to me, and I had the feeling she wasn't satisfied, either. But David obviously saw something through the lens that the rest of us weren't aware of." He dropped the sheaf of pictures on Adam's desk. "This woman comes alive for the camera. Look."

Adam pushed his other work aside and gave his attention to the glossies, scrutinizing them one by one. His face was unreadable, but he knew that Bill must have heard the sharp intake of his breath. What he saw stopped his heartbeat for an instant and sent it racing forward. The woman was sensational. Tina Lawrence, who had seemed ill at ease to him—just as she had to Bill and, he imagined, to Kay and even to herself—blossomed for David's camera. The lens loved every contour of her face, every angle, every curve. It captured and caressed each nuance of her expression. Adam reached the end of the stack and looked through it again, slowly this time, allowing his heart rate to return to normal. Then he glanced up at his ad manager and nodded.

"Look at these—the ones with Holly," Bill urged. "Like the feller says, you ain't seen nothin' yet."

Adam looked. The first thing that struck him, after the resemblance—which was even more notable than he'd expected—was the way that Tina and Holly complemented each other. Considering that Tina had been obviously nervous and Holly outwardly hostile, it was remarkable. They were pros, no doubt about that. But there was something more. Tina's maturity and serenity contrasted in a amazingly compatible way with Holly's youth and verve. Each seemed to bring out some hidden aspect of the other. It was more than he'd hoped for, more than anyone could have expected, this hidden magic that came so rarely.

"Well?" Bill prodded.

Adam let the pictures fall to his desk as he got up and began his pacing, which today seemed more like that of a cat on the prowl. In a familiar gesture, he ran his hand through his hair and then frowned unexpectedly. Bill didn't miss the expression.

"Everything's all right, except for whatever it is that's wrong, right?" Bill said enigmatically. "Where's the problem?" He seemed to know his employer very well indeed.

"The Carlson thing. It still worries me the way she left that campaign." Adam paused in midstride and looked at Bill. "Have you heard any more?"

"It's an old story, and the rumor mill isn't interested at this point in reviving it," he replied. "You could always call Carlson . . ."

"Hardly," Adam said in a manner that his ad manager had expected. "Do you know anyone over there?"

"I've been dating a girl whose sister works for Carlson."

"That's good enough. Find out what happened. Did Bettina break a contract or was it a legal problem or just a misunderstanding? Did Carlson overreact? Apparently there was a hell of a lot of talk. Why did she really leave?" Adam was thinking aloud while Bill made mental notes. "There must be plenty of jealous models around from back then who'd be willing to talk about it. Find me some answers."

"So we hold off the decision..."

"I didn't say that." Adam sat back down at his desk and glanced through the pictures one more time, trying to push aside his nagging doubts about Tina's stability and concentrate on her uncanny likeness to Holly and her magical indescribable quality.

"Should I have the rest of the team take a look at the pictures?" Bill referred to the other creative people at Century's in-house agency.

"No," Adam answered as he studied the photographs through narrowed eyes. He hadn't gotten where he was by asking the advice of others or by being cautious. When he'd played football, Adam had never hesitated to run the ball himself when no receiver was open, dodging tackles with lightning-quick moves. He was known as a man who loved risks, and he was known as a winner. The question remained: was Tina Lawrence a winner?

Adam looked up from the pictures. "I think we'll hold a press conference."

"What?" Bill was a little confused. Had the decision been made? "You're going to hire her?"

"Correct."

Bill paused for a beat. "But you still want the research—Carlson, contract and all the rest?"

"Right again. I want to know what I'm up against before we leave her open for the press. I don't want any surprises."

"I can talk to Kay Cooper and David Stern, too," Bill suggested.

"Forget them; they're friends. Find some enemies. Meanwhile get the contracts over to Kay's office today. And tell Miss Lawrence to drop some weight—about ten pounds, I should think. She's photographing heavy." He kept the words deliberately harsh to counteract the excitement he felt just looking at her face, a face that wasn't brittle and fake but alive and almost sweet—and somehow rather sad.

As Bill unwound himself from his slouching position and stood up, Adam continued to think aloud. "Fix her up at that club of Holly's—what's it called?"

"Aquarius, I think."

"Have her make an appointment with the guy who takes Holly through the workout." Adam was already organizing a script to make sure that everything went the way he wanted with no snags. There would be only one quarterback in this campaign, and that was indisputably Adam Cole. "Now, about the press conference. Set it up for Thursday. A big bash." The orders were coming staccato fast now, but Bill wasn't missing a one. "Rent space at the St. Moritz. I want plenty of food and liquor. First class. But I want to know about her first—all about her—so we don't have any bombshells. This one got to the top and couldn't stay there, retired and couldn't hack it. We may have to *make* a winner out of her."

Bill was smiling as he left the office. "This is going to be one hell of a campaign, Adam."

"It better be," Adam said as he turned his attention back to the work on his desk. Or tried to. His eyes and his mind kept wandering to the photographs. There was something about Tina Lawrence that reached out to him even through the pictures. He'd felt it when he met her at the studio. Barefoot, in a dress that was all wrong, shy, she'd seemed more like an ingenue trying out for an amateur theatrical production. But when he touched her he'd felt her warmth. It had seeped through his fingertips as they rested on her hair and her face, and it had confused him. Maybe that's why he'd lashed out, making that remark about her off-the-farm look. It had been cruel, but it had been necessary to stop the tenderness that he'd felt when he touched her. Adam pushed the papers aside and buzzed his secretary. "No calls for a while," he commanded. He wanted to think.

He'd been nervous, too, at the shooting. His career was riding on this campaign, and his choices were going to have to be right. Of course, they would be; they'd never failed him before, but still something had made him assert his authority that morning, and it was nerves.

Well, the die was cast now. Adam walked over to the window and looked out on the perfect autumn day. He and Tina were bound together—along with Holly. Adam had no qualms about his daughter. Even after the fight they'd had about her mother in the limo the morning of the shooting, she'd been able to pull the session off. Holly was a winner. She'd proven herself. But what about Tina Lawrence...what about Bettina?

Winning was very important to Adam Cole. From the time he played his first football game on the vacant lot near his house in Meadville, Pennsylvania, he'd known he was a winner, sensed it with a child's deep intuition. He was good in all sports, but he excelled in football. Quick, agile and strong, he was a natural leader, and he quarterbacked every team he played on from the vacant lot to the pros.

Adam remembered the day he won his scholarship to the university. His parents' pride had been almost uncontrollable. His father, born Pavlo Kowalsky, the son of an immigrant steelworker, truly believed in the

American way. Yet he'd never expected more than a decent job, a house to live in and food on the table. When Adam won the scholarship to play football, it was like a miracle. Pavlo was filled with pride and humility that such good fortune had come to their family. His life hadn't been very easy, and it wasn't destined to be very long, but Pavlo lived to see Adam become All-American and sign his multimillion dollar contract with the Erie Lakers.

Adam moved his mother to Florida then so she could escape the Pennsylvania cold that made her arthritis even more painful in the long winter months. Adam's brothers and sisters had scattered, making lives of their own, and Adam, too, had begun thinking of getting married. There wasn't any question of his choice.

He met Pam Jensen standing in line at the student-union building his freshman year at college. The meeting appeared accidental. Pam had seen to that. She wasn't wealthy, but compared to the Kowalsky family the Jensens were well-off, and Pam hadn't really worked for anything or wanted for anything in her life until she saw Adam Cole striding across the campus.

"Who is he?" she whispered to her roommate. "He's the most beautiful man I've ever seen."

Pam found out, and within a week she'd managed the meeting at the student union, which resulted in their first date. They were totally different. She was fair and blond; he was dark. She was laid back; he was motivated. She was polished; he was rough, but in his roughness Pam found an aura of excitement, a glamour that prophesied a big future for the football star.

She wanted him, and Pam usually got what she wanted.

They were married the year before Adam graduated and went into the pros. By then he knew that she'd staged their first meeting, and he could only be grateful. Pam was just what he needed, a girl with a sense of style, self-assurance and what he could only call class. The girls he'd grown up with had been a little awkward and unsure and not at all sophisticated. Pam always knew the right thing to do and say.

Her influence was subtle, but it brought about changes in Adam that were slow at first and then became a part of him. The changes began in his choice of clothes and then his hairstyle, in the wines he learned to enjoy and the restaurants he frequented. The beer-and-hamburger days were gone for good, replaced by champagne and caviar and never for a moment regretted.

Adam signed with the Erie Lakers, pulling in the biggest bonus in the annals of pro football, and later that same year Holly was born. Pam thought her life was complete; she had Adam, a beautiful baby daughter, more money than she knew what to do with and a life-style that equaled any movie star's.

The life-style lasted until his injury, which sidelined him for a year and then forced him to retire. At the age of thirty-one, Adam began to look around for something else to do. Money wasn't an immediate problem, since his advisers had invested wisely for him, but he was worried about how to spend the rest of his life. He needed a challenge. Then he heard about Century Cosmetics.

He and Pam began having their first arguments during the early months with Century, quarrels that led eventually to the breakdown of their marriage. Adam had never stopped in his drive. He'd pushed himself to get ahead in football so he could have everything he wanted. Then he'd continued pushing so he could keep it. When football was over he'd put all his energies into getting ahead in business—and staying there.

And why not, he often asked Pam when she complained about his long hours. She had needs—and luxuries, plenty of them—that she couldn't do without. What had she expected from him—miracles? Had she wanted him to create a Cinderella company and then go jet-setting around the world with her, spending wildly until there was nothing left? Well, remaking a business and keeping on top was a full-time job. A week now and then for a cruise or a trip abroad was all right, but he didn't have any more time than that to waste. Even if he made all the money he needed or ever wanted, slowing down was out of the question. Adam had to have a challenge; without the challenge, there was nothing, he was nothing. All that he told her before the end.

By then she'd stopped listening. By then they weren't really talking, they were arguing, and that only during the rare moments when Adam left his work to come home. "You won't even know I'm gone," she told him before she finally left for good, walking out and heading for Europe and a life-style that attracted her like a glittering bauble.

In a way, she was right. Adam spent sixteen hours a day at Century, and he didn't have time for hurt. But he took time to wage a long court battle to keep his daughter with him, accusing Pam of desertion. Then he put the pain aside, not thinking about it, burying it in his work. But never in the four years since the divorce had he been able to forget the bitterness.

Holly had already decided that she wanted to model, and Adam saw no reason not to agree. Without completely understanding what was going on inside this beautiful twelve-year-old creature who was his daughter, he suspected that Holly was lonely without her mother. She needed someone or something to cling to; she needed to keep busy.

Adam crossed to the corner of his office, poured a cup of coffee and wondered if he'd been wrong to encourage Holly's career. She seemed to enjoy it, but he wasn't sure that he enjoyed watching what it was doing to her. He grimaced at the remembrance of her haughty scene with Tina. There'd been more and more of that behavior recently, causing him to wonder what had turned his daughter into a girl who'd become uncommunicative at best, sullen at worst. He'd given her the Generations Girl because he'd hoped it would bring them closer.

Holly seemed to think otherwise. "You want me for Generations because I'm hot," she'd told him. "I'm a sure thing. It has nothing to do with us working together and sharing something—all that stuff you told me when you decided I could do it. It's just because I'm at the top, that's all." She'd screamed at him, leaving Adam shaking his head. Kids. They had the craziest ideas about their worth. Of course, she was the best teenage model in the country today, and that was certainly one of the reasons he'd agreed to let her do the job. But he wasn't using her. He was ambitious, but not that ambitious.

Where Tina Lawrence was concerned, however, there were no extenuating circumstances; he was going with her because she was right. As if drawn by a magnet, Adam returned to the desk and let his eyes flick over the glossy photos. There was no attachment as with Holly, but there was plenty of risk. He was taking a big chance. No one in the company, not even Bill, his closest confidant, knew how much was riding on the success of this line. He'd drawn money from the other holdings and mortgaged property when research and development on the new line went way over budget. Yet he'd chosen Tina Lawrence without hesitation.

Adam sat down and sifted through the pictures again, asking himself why he'd done it. Part of the reason was her look, the look that blended so well with Holly's, but that wasn't all. He'd wanted to touch her as soon as he'd seen her. That had unnerved him. So he'd quickly established his control. Or tried to. Her smile at the end of the session, her look, had told him that he hadn't quite succeeded.

For the first time since he could remember, Adam felt confused by a woman. No woman had made him feel unsure of himself—ever. And he certainly hadn't been seriously involved with anyone since Pam. Instead there'd been a long line of women who were no more than adornments for his arm. With just one look, a few words and an unforgettable smile, Tina Lawrence had let him know that she wasn't going to be an adornment.

Adam put the pictures aside, this time for the rest of the morning, he told himself as he buzzed his secretary again, asking her to let the calls come through. In the past, Adam had always relied on his instincts to make decisions. His instincts had told him to go with Tina Lawrence, but he was beginning to wonder if the reasons were the right ones. If they weren't he could be making a big mistake.

"I'm telling you, she's just what she seems. There's no scandal left," Bill Fontana said to Adam when they met in the lobby of the St. Moritz Hotel. The press conference was an hour away; everything was ready.

"What about Carlson?"

"He overreacted, from everything I can tell," Bill assured him.

"She wasn't committed?"

"Well, yes and no. They'd settled on her, and Kay had cleared her schedule, but she left before signing a contract. Apparently Carlson was livid. At the time there was a lot of talk, but now, after all these years, even the ones who were willing to believe anything say old Carlson instigated most of the rumors."

"Then why the hell did she leave?" Adam was impatient.

"She fell in love and escaped with the guy to the mountains of Colorado."

"That's it?"

"That's it."

Adam smiled. She was impetuous; he'd known that. They would have to keep an eye on her, but as far as the press questions were concerned, there was nothing to fear. "I think I'll take charge of the press conference until someone asks her about the past. Then I'll give her rein. I have a feeling her answer will make my day. Come on; let's get to the ballroom. I can't wait for this event to begin." Adam Cole loved a good show, especially if it ended in victory; today, he anticipated, the victory would be very sweet indeed.

"Do you think I'll pass inspection?" Tina couldn't resist a little sarcasm as she did a full turn in front of Kay.

"You look sensational. It's amazing what a decent haircut can achieve. Who did your hair in Colorado?"

Tina smiled, giving a shake to her long thick hair and watching it in the mirror above Kay's sofa as it fell back in perfect waves to her shoulders, the result of two hours with Kay's hairdresser. "No one *did* my hair. Sometimes Eli cut it for me."

"Who's he?"

"Eli's a she. She and Kam are my strong right hands at the inn. They came the winter that Bryant died, and they do everything for me—"

"Including giving you a haircut with the kitchen shears," Kay commented before adding, "The dress is perfect."

Glancing in the mirror again, Tina couldn't help but agree. "But are you sure it doesn't make me look too fat? I wouldn't want Mr. Cole to be upset," she said sweetly.

Kay glanced up quickly from the press release that she was reading. "Cynicism doesn't become you, honey. Adam was only saying what you already knew—and what I'd already told you."

"Yes, but from you it sounded... well, friendly. From him it was downright domineering."

Kay refused to be drawn into conflict between Tina and the man who was paying the bills. "Adam Cole is very determined, and this campaign is important to him. Make no mistake about it, he plans for nothing short of perfection," she said, ending the conversation but not ending Tina's concern—which had become almost obsessive, Tina admitted to herself as she walked closer to the mirror to admire her first good haircut in years.

The tension between her and Adam Cole had been palpable. It had bothered her then; it worried her now. She had the feeling that he wanted to take over her life, wanted in some sort of perverse way to control her. That didn't go with the job, she told herself.

Tina remembered Bill Fontana's call to say that she'd been chosen and the contracts were on the way, but the momentary balloon of pleasure that went up for her was immediately popped by Adam Cole's interference. "By the way," Bill had said, "Adam wants you to lose a little weight. In fact, he made a referral for you..."

Tina had written down the name and address and stuffed it in her handbag with no intention of taking it further. She'd lose weight in her own way with her own exercise program. She decided not to mention that little bit of rebellion to Kay, whose face now appeared behind her in the mirror. "Come on, Cinderella, your coach is waiting."

"Well, let's hope it doesn't turn into a pumpkin," Tina said breezily to cover her nervousness over what lay ahead.

But Kay was wise to her. "Don't worry," she continued in the same playful vein. "There won't be any wicked stepsisters among the press."

Tina laughed but couldn't control a little shiver at the approach of her first appearance before the press since she'd fled New York. How many would remember her? And how many of those who did remember would be friendly?

"My Lord, you are spectacular." Adam's eyes drank in Tina from her shining hair to her silvery spike-heeled sandals that brought her within two inches of his height.

"I should be," Tina replied. "You paid enough for all this." As instructed, she'd charged everything to Century, from her haircut to her facial and manicure and, of course, the designer dress—and even the wispy lingerie beneath it. Tina watched as his eyes took in the dress, chosen carefully to highlight her every asset, and she had the feeling he was trying to identify the unusual fabric. It was Italian, handwoven and soft as silk but with more texture so that the folds of the scooped neck fell dramatically to her breasts. The skirt was slit to her knee, and as she walked, her long legs were whispers of silk. When she turned toward Bill Fontana, who was beckoning to them from the doorway, her hair glowed fiery red against the quicksilver-colored dress.

Adam must have seen Bill motioning to them, but his gaze, frankly candid, remained on Tina, and she realized that she was enjoying every moment of this sudden admiration. It almost masked the nervousness that coursed through her. Almost.

Finally, Adam slipped his hand beneath her bare smooth arm and led her to the door, walking close to her, as if he belonged there. Tina moved away slightly, but his grip remained firm, keeping her within his sphere of control.

Adam had chosen to throw the press party early in the evening so they'd make the eleven-o'clock news and the morning papers. He noticed in the crowd stringers from the major newspapers and editors from all the fashion magazines, and he was pleased. The turnout proved that he still had the power to garner publicity. Of course, he admitted, if only to himself, the name Bettina hadn't hurt.

Holly was dressed in bright silk paneled with purple, parrot green and sunshine yellow. Her hair was brushed up on the sides and then brought forward over her forehead. She looked adorably pouty. It was a preening pout, however, something like that of a glittering bird of paradise, and as they stood silently for the photographers, Tina was glad she hadn't tried to compete.

When the picture-taking session ended, they joined Bill and Adam at a long table facing the press. Adam took charge immediately, explaining the Generations line, which he believed to be a new concept in makeup. "While other companies have introduced products for both teenage and mature skin, we're the first to make this sort of concentrated effort to pamper the skin at each stage of a woman's life, changing as she matures," he added, purposefully avoiding the use of the word *ages*. "Century Cosmetics is responsive to her changes, and our products—makeup and facial care— have all been researched and designed to take every change into consideration."

Bill Fontana then described the years of research to get the products ready for the market, beginning shortly after Adam joined the small, highly respected cosmetics company and by long hours of hard work, single-mindedness of purpose and personal involvement expanded it into a major corporation. As Bill spoke about Adam, Tina glanced briefly at Holly to see the girl's face tighten. Then she realized that Holly had paid some of the price for Adam's empire.

Tina had known plenty of men like him, driven toward success at any cost. Adam fit the mold perfectly. Certainly, he was in control tonight, darkly handsome in his custom-made dinner jacket, tanned, hair perfectly styled. Yet there was a difference between him and other executives that some people never noticed but that Tina had already discerned. Under the well-cut clothes was a brawny man who'd fought hard to be successful and in spite of his aura of classiness, didn't care who knew it.

Adam was speaking again, getting to the point of the press conference by explaining that he was initiating a media blitz with a multimillion-dollar budget, and for that kind of exposure he'd hired the very best.

"You can't say I don't believe in nepotism at Century." He glanced at Holly with a smile as laughter floated across the elegant room. "But she also happens to be the most beautiful young model working today, my daughter, Holly Cole." Holly stood up to a ripple of applause, and then she did something that Tina didn't expect. She reached over and took her father's hand. It was a touching moment, Tina thought, but a little too staged not to have been rehearsed.

Next Adam turned his attention to Tina. "All of you remember her," he said. "She was at the top, the standard of beauty by which others were measured, and we are fortunate to have lured her back to New York for the Century campaign." He paused and looked at Tina with such force and such feeling that she felt an unaccustomed blush rise to her cheeks. Apparently this was what he'd wanted, for he smiled and said quietly, "May I present—Bettina."

This time the applause was long and loud, and the questions that followed were as friendly as the wel-

come. However she wasn't allowed more than a few
words of response to any question before Adam
jumped in with his own explanation and edification,
as if he feared that she would make a mistake. She was
beginning to imagine that he had taken her for a total
fool when the question was asked that she had been
expecting—and fearing.

The woman who asked it was an editor with a major fashion magazine. Tina had known her in the old
days and thought the woman liked her. Maybe she did;
maybe the question just had to be asked.

"Some of us old-timers—" there was a pause for
polite laughs of denial "—some of us remember the
Carlson campaign and your walking out. Have you
talked to Mr. Carlson recently?"

"No . . ." Tina said, aware that more was coming.

"Well, I have." The editor was as thin as a model
herself, with dark hair pulled back in a tight bun, a
dress of solid black and lips that were a slash of red.
Her voice was low and harsh, what old-timers called
a whiskey voice—and for good reason. "Mr. Carlson
is still angry over that campaign. He insinuated that
you might pull the same thing again." The woman's
red lips formed a bright smile. "So I'll ask you personally. Can you stick it out this time, Bettina, or will
you run away again?"

Tina waited for a beat, expecting Adam to jump in.
When he made no move to answer for her, she spoke.

"I left New York almost ten years ago. I left hur-
riedly and perhaps thoughtlessly. But I was in love,"
she said, "and I had to get on with my life." She didn't
mention Carlson again or apologize or even try to de-
fend herself. That was past history; Tina wanted to
talk about now. "I've come back, a stronger and I

hope a wiser person—obviously an older one." She smiled a disarming smile, wondering how she managed to be so calm when inside she was trembling like a leaf.

"But I've come back," she continued, "for one purpose—to work on the Generations campaign. When that is over, I'll return to Colorado. Not before."

From the back of the room, a male voice, tired of the questions and looking forward to the refreshments, called out, "We're glad you're back, Bettina," and Bill Fontana used the moment to bring everything to an end.

"I think we're ready for the party. On behalf of Century Cosmetics, let me thank you all for coming. There's a buffet in the back, and the bar is now open."

As the crowd filed out, Adam turned to Tina. "Thanks," he said softly. "You handled that well."

"It's all part of the package you paid for, Mr. Cole. I want this campaign to succeed as much as you. My image is involved, too." She didn't mention the way he'd answered for her until the end; she assumed it was part of a plan, and she couldn't complain. Like all of his plans, it worked.

"Please call me Adam." His hand reached out to touch her waist. She could feel its strength and warmth through the thin fabric of her dress. "After the party, I'd like for you to stay at the St. Moritz and have dinner with me. Since we're going to be working together closely, we should get to know each other better." There was admiration in his eyes and a flicker of something else that Tina recognized quickly. She avoided it and smiled her most charming smile.

"Thank you, Mr. Cole, but I plan to miss both the buffet and the dinner tonight. I've been warned that I'm a little overweight and must avoid indulging. I imagine that means even with the boss. Now if you'll excuse me, I see an old friend from *Vogue*." She turned on her silvery heel and glided through the throng.

Adam stood looking after her, admiration still flickering in his eyes even after her refusal. She was a challenge, and Adam Cole thrived on challenges.

Chapter 4

The Aquarius Health Club occupied the top floor of an office building on the east side of Manhattan. It looked less like a gym, Tina thought, than a hothouse. The workout area was festooned with enormous plants dripping over shelves, hanging from the ceiling, spilling out of every corner, lit by artificial light and spritzed lovingly and daily by a faithful attendant. The glass-domed areas were even more luxurious, since they had been constructed a level below, on the actual rooftop of the skyscraper. The women's spa was on the front side with a view across the United Nations Plaza to the East River. Under the dome, the spa plants had a jump on those inside, fed as they were by the sun and the steam.

On Tina's first visit she'd almost balked when she saw the pink-and-green striped lobby with white wicker furniture, pink and green pillows, plants everywhere and a vivacious receptionist wearing a brief

Aquarius smock. At least that wasn't pink and green, Tina had thought as she let herself be led in for an obligatory tour before signing up. She'd managed to get through the introduction, a demonstration of the weight machines, the free weights and the bicycles, a promenade around the spa and locker room and finally an introduction to the inimitable Paul Watson.

Paul had been designated to get Tina into shape in three weeks and make sure she stayed there throughout the Generations campaign. He looked as though he was up to the task, if the muscles that bulged under his Aquarius T-shirt were any indication of his worth. His skin was clean, smooth and lightly tanned; his hair was equally clean, crisp and well styled; his eyes were bright—they even sparkled. He was the picture of health. Tina groaned silently.

She'd been determined not to end up at the club Adam Cole had suggested, simply because, like all his suggestions, it had been more akin to an order if not a royal decree. However, in asking around, Tina had discovered that Aquarius and Paul were precisely what she needed to get back into shape in the limited time that was available. So she'd reluctantly turned herself over to the pink-and-green fantasy called Aquarius, only to find that it was very real indeed, painfully so.

Paul had put her on a diet that included small meals throughout the day—never quite enough, as far as Tina was concerned. She was used to eating a huge breakfast at the inn and then working all day, often missing lunch or grabbing a candy bar and soft drink in the middle of the afternoon and finally sitting down—late, after the guests had eaten—to another of Kam's filling meals, often including fried steak and potatoes.

"No more of that," Paul had told her. "You have to treat your calories like money—spread them around." The nibbles he suggested six times a day were a little too health-foody for Tina's taste, but because she was always starving she'd begun to look forward to the bran and grain and vegetables. She didn't even fuss anymore about the water flavored with two tablespoons of orange juice, which was her treat at the end of a workout. In fact, it began to taste damned good after she stumbled away from her last weight-lifting machine.

Even with sore muscles, Tina admitted that she felt better—and looked better. The sags were beginning to lift a little, and her complexion glowed.

"Even your hair is glossier," Paul told a somewhat disbelieving Tina. "It's not the shampoo and conditioners and packs you put on it, believe me; it's what you put in your body. Remember, we are what we eat."

Now, at the end of her second week of training, Tina thought she'd heard them all. She'd made it to the last machine again—the double-shoulder—when he threw out that one, and she almost lost her beat. "Oh, Paul, please. I can't stand any more maxims."

"No talking. Just listen. Eleven," he counted. "That's a girl. Hyperextend—all the way back as far as you can go. Twelve. Good. Push slowly. Push. That's it. Thirteen. One more. All right!"

"Am I free?" Tina managed to gasp, wiping her face with the towel around her neck.

"You're free. Into the whirlpool. Then a sauna and a cold shower, and you're a new woman. Oh, don't forget your orange water," he added with a grin, handing Tina the bottle as she headed for the women's spa.

By the time she got to the locker room, stripped off her leg warmers and unitard and wrapped herself in a towel, she'd finished the whole bottle. Tossing it into the trash, she tugged the towel securely around her and headed across the pink-and-green tiled floor for the hot tub.

Settling blissfully into the steaming water, she leaned back with a sigh and looked through the skylight at the clouds scudding across the September sky. Her session with Paul had been a good one. He'd been right about her glow. She felt the benefits of each workout not only physically, in the tightening of her stomach muscles, firming up of her thighs and upper arms, but—just as he'd reminded her—in an overall healthy appearance. Every time Tina looked in the mirror, she was surprised at the change she saw there. But Paul's biggest accomplishment was her emotional good health. She was more relaxed. Shooting on Generations began in a week, and Tina was almost ready.

Thinking about the past two weeks she wondered if Paul—or someone like him—could have gotten her through the burnout she'd experienced in New York years earlier. Probably not, she decided. Now everything seemed so much easier, more relaxed and less pressured, maybe because she was older and, as she'd suggested at the press conference, more mature. At any rate, she didn't have to prove herself over and over this time—only once, and she was ready for that. When the campaign ended, she could go home to Colorado, and no one would call it running away. Tina gave herself to the bubbles, dreamily, not thinking about anything now, just floating.

A sudden splash washed over her, and she came up sputtering to find Holly Cole beside her in the pool. Tina hadn't seen Holly since the press conference, when they'd barely exchanged more than a smile. That is, *she'd* smiled. If she recalled correctly, Holly had pouted. At their only other encounter, the day they'd met, the girl had been frankly rude. Tina felt no compunction to make overtures to Holly now, remembering that meeting that still rankled her.

She closed her eyes again, but common sense prevailed. They'd be working together, long hours in very intense sessions, and she'd lose nothing by making another attempt with the girl—who *was* a child, Tina reminder herself, even if in looks and outward sophistication she seemed like a grown woman.

"Hi," Tina said through the steam.

Holly looked at her out of the corner of her eye, as if surprised that she'd spoken. "Oh, it's you," she said, and Tina realized that the girl hadn't even recognized her. She wondered if Holly ever gave a second glance to anyone—except herself.

"Yes," Tina said, still determined. "I knew you worked out at Aquarius, but I don't believe I've seen you here in the mornings."

Holly submerged inch by careful inch while she apparently tried to decide whether she would respond or not. Finally she managed, "No, I'm usually here at night." Not another word was forthcoming, and Tina had just about decided to try once more when half the aerobics class entered the spa and one by one plunged into the hot tub, moaning and groaning about their workouts. When the last—and largest—of the group plopped in beside them, creating a minor tidal wave, Tina caught Holly's eyes and thought she discerned a twinkle there, but she wasn't sure and finally decided to forget the challenge. They were both pros; they could work together without being friends. Besides, she'd never been overly crazy about teenage girls and their hangups.

As the tub got more crowded, Tina slipped out and into the steam room. Twenty minutes later, after the steam and her required cold shower, she went into the locker room to find that the crowd had left except for a few stragglers still putting final touches on their makeup—and Holly, who was sitting on a bench sipping a diet drink.

Tina smiled at her again on the way to the lockers but didn't bother to try another conversation. That's why she was so startled when the girl called out to her, "Paul said you were his favorite pupil."

Tina turned around, "What?"

"He did," Holly repeated in a manner that was almost little-girlish. "You work harder than anyone, and you're also more beautiful. That's what he said. I believe he has a thing for you."

Tina laughed, still wondering why the girl had suddenly decided to talk and imagining that she'd never find out—assuming there was a reason other than teenage moodiness.

"He's very good," Tina answered, "but, oh, my aching muscles."

"I know," Holly said. "He's a demon. Has he made a pass at you yet?"

"Holly! No," Tina said quickly.

"Well, he will. Paul likes older women—not that you're old, but you know what I mean."

"Well, I'm almost thirty-six, and I do know what you mean."

"Are you really? Thirty-six? You don't look that old, and Paul's right, you're really beautiful." Holly was still sitting on the bench toweling her damp hair. She looked about twelve, Tina thought, wrapped in a towel with no makeup, vulnerable and rather sweet. She obviously was making an effort to be friendly. Tina decided to grab the moment in case it didn't happen again for a while.

"Thanks for the compliment."

"Let's have something to drink in the canteen after we get dressed," Holly suggested.

Tina glanced at the drink in Holly's hand and the girl giggled. "Don't tell Paul. I'm not supposed to have diet drinks, but I cheat. At the canteen, I'll get carrot juice in case he walks in."

Half an hour later Holly was ready, or so she said, although her hair, blown dry and flying wildly in all directions, looked to Tina as if it could use a little taming. Her clothes, too, were wild—an oversized shirt, paisley pants and a striped vest, pink knee socks and red lace-up shoes. It was an outfit, Tina mused, designed to attract attention, even among blasé New Yorkers, but if Holly had worn it for that reason, it didn't show in her manner. Obviously she'd thrown the separates together with some thought to the ultimate effect, but now that she had them on, they were forgotten. She wasn't modeling today; she was just being Holly—take it or leave it, her look said. Tina couldn't help but be impressed. The girl was sassy but, when she wanted to be, likable.

Holly smiled at the attendant behind the counter. "I'll have a tofu burger, cashew chicken salad, a dish of yogurt with strawberries and a double carrot juice."

"Good Lord, Holly—" Tina began.

"Well, it's all healthy."

When she joined Tina at the table after collecting her order, she'd already finished the strawberries and yogurt.

"I thought Paul's advice was several small meals a day," Tina said, looking somewhat enviously at the plates of food.

"Hmm. But I'm hyperactive or something. I can eat like a horse and never gain weight. Paul just tries to make sure that I eat healthy stuff instead of candy and cake and soft drinks—all that food I *really* like. I'm sorry I was rude that day on the set," Holly threw in from left field.

"That's all right," Tina said, a little stunned.

"I'm not so good at meeting new people. I don't know what to say and all. You know. That's the way I am," she added without apology. At barely sixteen, she certainly knew herself well, Tina thought. "I was a witch at the shooting, right?"

Tina sipped her juice and then took a bite of her small vegetable salad without answering, and Holly went right on. "I'd just had a huge fight with my dad in the car, and I was ready to hate everybody. On top of that, I'd had sessions with about ten million models for the Generations casting, and I was really getting tired of it. So—I'm sorry. And I'm glad they picked you," she added.

"Apology accepted—and thanks," Tina responded. She remembered her own teenage years, her ups and downs and mood swings. In a way Holly was just like other girls her age—only more so, with every mood taken as far as it could go because she was also a star and the limits were much higher. Holly was no fool; she knew what she could get away with. But under the image of glossy model, Tina was relieved to see there was a relatively normal kid with real emotions.

"I'll bet the fight was about a boyfriend," Tina guessed, remembering again her youthful disagreements with her parents—and the usual reasons for them.

Holly drained her carrot juice. "No, it was about my mom." Her face closed around that sentence with the same expression Tina had seen at the press conference when Bill had been talking about her father's dedication to his work. Seeing the strain put on the girl by the mention of parents, Tina wisely didn't pursue the subject further.

"Well, just so it wasn't because of me. I'm nervous enough about the Generations campaign."

Holly's blue eyes widened to an impossibly large size. "You are?" She was startled by that revelation. "But you were terrific. I saw the glossies. We looked great together." Her manner in mentioning that was unaffected. Holly wasn't bragging; she was just stating a fact.

"Thanks, pal. I needed that." Tina reached over and in a purely instinctive gesture clasped Holly's hand. The girl's face reddened, and she quickly broke the contact, embarrassed either by Tina's display of gratitude or by the affection that went with it. After glancing at her Micky Mouse watch, Holly announced that she was late. "My tutor. Algebra—ugh." She grimaced dramatically.

"I sympathize," Tina said. "Which is all I can do, not being a math scholar."

"Who would want to be?" Holly wondered aloud as she stood up, threw her tote bag over her shoulder and smiled. "They'll never make one of me, either, no matter how hard they try," she vowed. "Well, this was fun. Let's work out together with Paul next time."

"I'd love to, but you're probably years ahead of me." Tina could visualize Holly's lithe body bending in every possible direction.

"So I'll slow down, and you'll speed up." Holly grinned, waved her fingers, calling out, "Later," and was gone.

Tina sat back, relieved that they'd had a chance to talk and if not become fast friends at least get on speaking terms. She watched Holly, a mismatched jumble of strange clothing and long body, disappear through the door and stretched out her own long, tired legs and finished her juice.

Tina had dressed more carefully than her counterpart today, wearing a pleated skirt, white blouse and navy blazer because her plans for the afternoon were conservative, far away from the high wire, and she was excited about what lay ahead.

However, her day was to have one more interruption from a member of the Cole family. The voice, which in a short time had become very familiar, came from behind her table.

"So you did take my advice?"

She turned slowly to face him before denying what he'd said. "I checked around, and Paul was the most highly recommended instructor."

Adam grinned, not a bit daunted by Tina's show of independence. "At the risk of sounding repetitive, you look quite wonderful again today."

She nodded her thanks.

"Different. Another image. Is this one the real you?" he asked rhetorically as he hooked a sneakered foot around the metal leg of a chair, pulled it toward him and sat down without benefit of invitation. Even dressed in corduroy shorts and a T-shirt he looked important, not just as if he belonged at Aquarius but as if he could have bought the club had the idea occurred to him.

Tina tried not to notice how the shirt molded tightly across his broad shoulders, but as he sat beside her, she couldn't avoid seeing the rippling muscles in his thighs or thinking that she'd never seen a man with such beautiful legs, long and lean and finely muscled, their only imperfection a deep scar on one knee. He smelled faintly of perspiration and tangy cologne and more strongly of masculinity.

"I was just getting ready to leave," she said, trying to prepare for the exit she very much wanted to make. "Holly left a few minutes ago; you just missed her."

Adam glanced at his watch. "She has a tutoring session."

"Yes, I'm sure she made it," Tina answered, wondering if Adam monitored all of his daughter's activities and deciding that he did, considering his need to be in control of everything and everyone within his sphere.

"Don't go yet," Adam said. "Stay and have a drink with me. I'm new here, too, but I hear that there's a bar on the level just below the club."

It wasn't exactly a demand, this remark, but she read it as one, maybe because of the way his eyes locked on hers and held as he spoke, almost making a prisoner of her. Trapped, that's how he made her feel, and it frightened her. She turned away to escape his eyes and managed to remind him, "I have to leave. I'm late for an appointment—downtown. Maybe another time."

She started to get up, but his hand caught her and held her just as moments before his eyes had held. She looked down at his hand on her arm. It was tanned and strong. He wore a gold signet ring on his little finger, and his nails were perfectly manicured. The warmth from his hand flowed to her, but it wasn't comforting; it was hot and demanding.

"Tonight," he said.

"What?"

"I'll see you tonight."

"I'm sorry, but—" she began before he interrupted her.

"I'm not talking about a social evening, Bettina."

At the use of her professional name, she jerked her head around to look at him, and this time she met his eyes evenly, pro to pro.

"If you'll read your contract," Adam went on, "you'll see you've agreed to certain publicity and promotional appearances. Tonight falls into that category."

She hesitated and then answered, "Of course." Tina *had* read the contract and remembered the publicity clause.

He moved his hand then, as if to let her escape—but only for now. "I'll pick you up around eight. Wear something spectacular," he added, "Long and slinky and sexy."

Not acknowledging the demand, she fumbled in her bag for a pen. "Let me give you my address."

"Not necessary." His white teeth gleamed against his tanned skin in a smile. "I know where you live. I arranged the sublet." He reached over and touched her cheek and again she felt the heat. "I'll see you at eight." He got up then and sauntered away as if, indeed, he owned not just the club but the rest of the world, as well.

Tina sat at the table for a moment longer, fuming. Damn the man, she thought, for invading every corner of her life. She should have known the sublet Kay suggested was too good to be true. Arranged by Adam Cole, it was probably kept for his girlfriends. Tina stood up suddenly, knocking over the juice glass and then looking around to see if anyone had noticed. Quickly she picked up the glass and put it on the table. Then she slung her bag over her shoulder and stamped out the door, through the pink-and-green lobby and onto the generic elevator, whose lack of color she almost welcomed. She'd deal with Kay and the little apartment hoax later. Right now she had something else on her mind, a plan that Adam Cole had no control over and would never even know about.

Leaving the building in the bright sunshine, Tina put on her oversized sunglasses and marched across the sidewalk. She stepped off the curb and walked halfway into the street, where she boldly hailed a cab, taking, she thought, New York in her hands. She didn't need to hang on to the arm of Adam Cole or anyone else to make her way in this city. Times had

changed. She could walk the high wire—*and* make
something of herself, as well. She fully intended to do
both.

A taxi screeched to a halt, and Tina got in. "Washington Square," she told the driver. "New York University."

"You're very lucky, Mrs. Harris. The fall semester
has already begun, but there's an opening in the class
you want—someone dropped out just yesterday." The
bespectacled advisor smiled across at Tina. "Dr. Forrester's class in English Poetry is the most popular
course in our adult-education curriculum," she said
with a satisfied smile.

"Well, I had to start somewhere, and that sounded
very interesting to me," Tina said a little nervously.
Under the gaze of the older woman with her heavy-framed glasses and high-necked wool dress, Tina felt
a little suspect, even though she'd dressed for the occasion. "I always wanted to take some night courses,
because I never went to college," she explained.

"I know, I know," the woman clucked. "So often
marriage seems to come first. And then, of course, the
children take so much time."

Tina didn't bother to correct the assumption.

"Then there comes a time when we begin to regret
the lack of formal education, and that's when programs such as this one emerge to meet those needs,"
she added with a certain amount of pride as she inspected the application form and Tina's check for the
class fee. "Everything seems to be in order." She
nodded with approval. "I know that you'll enjoy Dr.
Forrester's class. Now," she declared, producing a
folded map, "this is our campus." She made an X over

one of the buildings. "We are here," she said with satisfaction, "and here's where your class will meet."

Tina nodded as another X was added to mark the spot. "Your class meets Tuesday and Thursday at seven-thirty in the evening." She handed Tina the map and a computer card that would admit her to the class. "Good luck, Mrs. Harris, and welcom to NYU."

Tina left the office feeling like a schoolgirl who'd just finished her orientation—and it was a good feeling. Her decision to register for a class at NYU hadn't been a mere whim or a spur-of-the-moment decision. She'd been thinking about it for a long time—probably since she'd first begun to realize her mistake in bypassing an education for the glamour of becoming a New York model. But on the way to the top there'd been no extra time for school, and when she became successful, her free evenings had been reserved for catching up on lost sleep. After she moved to Colorado, Timberline had taken all her extra time and money. Now she had some of both, and Tina hadn't hesitated to sign up for a night course. Maybe it would be the beginning of a college education that she could continue when she returned to Colorado.

Whatever happened in the future, this class and her dreams of someday obtaining a degree would be her secret. She would share it with no one, and especially not Adam Cole.

He arrived at the apartment on East Fifty-ninth Street promptly at eight o'clock. She might have known he wouldn't be late, Tina thought as she answered the door—*not* wearing long, slinky or sexy as he'd suggested. Instead she'd chosen a cameo-colored cashmere dress with a cowl neck and long, tight-fitting

sleeves—all covered up except for the briefest glimpse
of neck and shoulders.

As he swept her into the limo and gave a West Side
address, Tina couldn't tell whether Adam was angry
or amused over her blithe refusal to follow orders.
Certainly he wasn't unaware. He'd looked carefully,
and a lifted eyebrow had been his response. Tina tried
not to notice that there was something in the way he
lifted his eyebrow that told her that if she wasn't
wearing long and slinky, she'd unwittingly managed
sexy.

Tina decided to maintain a businesslike approach to
the evening, vowing that through the publicity party
she would play a role and then when the party ended
the role would continue—until Adam deposited her on
the doorstep of the apartment he'd arranged for her.
The business attitude would start now, as the limo
headed across town.

"Is there anything special I should know about tonight?" she asked. "Any preparation?" She preferred to know what was ahead; Tina had always done
her homework.

Adam smiled. "No, everything's arranged. Just
hang on to my arm and look gorgeous."

Tina's grimace of disdain at that remark was hidden by the shadow of passing cars in the night, and for
the rest of the ride, she answered Adam's conversa-
tional questions politely but briefly. She instigated no
conversation of her own, however, and made no
comments unless asked. Adam continued to be
friendly and animated, ignoring the fact that she
wasn't joining in.

The limo crossed Broadway on Forty-seventh Street
and pulled up behind a line of other cars. Ahead Tina

could see the glare of klieg lights and the explosion of flashbulbs. She watched curiously for a few minutes; Adam, for the first time that evening, was silent.

Then she realized what was happening. "We're going to the theater?" Her voice was incredulous; the publicity party was nothing more than the opening of a Broadway show. Adam had obviously pulled a fast one on her, and there was no avoiding it now as the limo reached the entrance to the theater.

The door of the car opened and Adam took her hand to help her out. "What better way to get the attention of the press than to go where they are? And tonight they're at the theater. Smile, Bettina."

Tina did as she was told, smiling for celebrity watchers who lined the ropes along the sidewalk, smiling for the press cameras and TV cameras and tourist cameras. Adam stopped and turned, his arm around her, and she continued to smile, icily, during the long ninety seconds before the next car deposited its passengers into the limelight.

As they walked into the theater through the narrow passage lined with fans, Tina heard a woman's voice rise above the noise of the crowd. "It's Adam Cole. Who's he with—a movie star?"

Adam heard, too, and bent to whisper, "Tomorrow everyone will know—Bettina."

The show, a lively British comedy, had been a hit in London and was selling out in advance on Broadway, attracting a star-studded opening-night crowd, some in evening dress and black tie. Tina was definitely underdressed for the occasion, but it served him right, she decided, for perpetuating this ruse.

The flood of humanity swept them into the lobby, where the beautiful people mingled—actors, politicians, businessmen whose faces she recognized from gossip columns. Adam seemed to know them all, and they stopped to talk to him, to meet Tina and, no doubt, to appraise her. In the classic cashmere outfit, she expected to be looked at with disdain; instead, the women's eyes were envious, the men's frankly admiring.

As for Adam, his hand around her waist was proprietary; for the next three hours at least she belonged to Century Cosmetics, to Generations and, it must follow, to Adam Cole. But the way he looked down at her made it seem as if she was *all* his, and there was nothing she could do to separate the personal from the professional—at least, not in public.

Yet before the play was over, Tina was glad she'd come. All day she'd been trying to convince herself that she wasn't interested in an evening on the town, and only because of the terms of her contract would she comply with Adam's invitation. But even as she'd lectured herself, her heart had been pounding with excitement. The excitement took on a new dimension in the theater with Adam at her side. She couldn't begin to guess how long it had been since she'd seen a Broadway play, how many years since she'd been a part of a glittering opening night. By intermission she was entranced; by the final curtain she was on her feet with the rest of the audience. The play was a hit, and so was the evening. She'd forgotten all about Adam's tricking her into a date, and when he suggested a light supper afterward, Tina found herself unable to refuse.

Adam steered her toward Eighth Avenue to a small bistro, where a pianist played in the bar and a few couples danced on the minute floor. The maître d' settled them at a secluded table and without asking brought a bottle of champagne.

"Is this your usual order?" Tina asked.

"I called ahead," Adam answered, "since this was a special occasion."

Tina didn't question that remark, for fear that he would put a personal stamp on the evening with his answer. Instead, when he held up his glass and his eyes met hers in that capturing, dark-eyed gaze, she said, "To Generations."

"Of course," Adam repeated. "Generations."

Tina took the first sip. The champagne was dry, bubbly and very expensive. "It's marvelous," she declared. "In fact, the whole evening has been marvelous." She smiled across at him, and something in his face made her catch her breath. She tried to tell herself that his look was one of approval at what he saw or possibly even gratitude at what she said, but she knew instantly and with absolute certainty that the look meant something else. It was so sexual that it could have been a look through eyes that saw her nude, lying in bed, rather than properly covered with cashmere, properly seated at a bistro table.

Tina knew that she had to say something now to stop what was happening and keep the rest of the evening light if not businesslike. She put down her glass and said with a touch of humor, "In spite of the success of the evening, I still have a feeling I was blackmailed into dinner with you."

"And if you were?" The look had gone from his eyes, which were simply inquisitive now, Tina saw with relief.

"Then I hope the dinner is a good one."

Adam's face broke into a grin. "Trust me, Tina. It will be. As for the blackmail, publicity about us attending this opening will be good for Generations. Besides, I thought it was time for us to get acquainted, have a long talk before the campaign begins. We'll be working very closely together. I plan to attend most of the shootings."

Tina didn't respond, but she wasn't at all surprised to hear that.

"So this seemed like a good opportunity for our talk, and if I had to use subterfuge to get you here, well, the end justifies the means, doesn't it?"

"Not always," Tina disputed, "but as for tonight, I had a good time. I'm still having a good time."

"That's all that matters," Adam said as he filled her glass again.

"I hadn't realized how much I missed some things."

"Like?"

"Oh, the excitement of an opening, the taste of good champagne. Just little things like that," she teased, "which aren't exactly a part of the daily grind at Timberline Inn."

"Tell me about your life out there," he said.

Tina hadn't meant to answer that so easily; she hadn't meant to let the conversation get personal. But somehow it seemed right, on this night in this little restaurant that was so full of quiet charm, to talk about her other life. So she told him all about the inn and Kam and Eli, their trials and tribulations, which she managed to make amusing.

Adam saw beneath the humor, and the questions he asked were pertinent, intelligent, probing. He seemed to care about her life in the Rockies; he seemed to understand it. And that's what she found so strange, coming from Adam Cole—who was, let's face it, Tina told herself, a swinger. Yet she wasn't so naive that she couldn't detect the difference between a man who was making a play and one who was interested. Tina smiled to herself; Adam Cole was both.

When he regaled her with stories of the football world followed by the world of cosmetics, Tina, too, was fascinated. He'd lived an exciting life; he was still living it, to the hilt. It was a life both hardworking and self-indulgent. She'd been there once and hadn't been comfortable; he was perfectly comfortable. He belonged at the top.

Not until after dinner, over coffee and brandy, did they talk about their marriages. Tina hadn't meant to do that, either, but she also hadn't meant for this evening to end alone at a bistro with Adam Cole. "Bryant was my refuge," she admitted. "I wanted to leave New York and get away from the rat race. He helped me." Then she smiled a smile of memory. "That sounds like we married to escape, but it wasn't that way at all. We were very close from the beginning; the decision to go to Colorado came later."

"But once it was made, there was apparently no hesitation. You walked out on the Carlson campaign for a new life."

Tina nodded.

Adam slowly stirred his coffee. "A little impetuous but not without purpose. A romantic gesture for home and family rather than career. Are you still a romantic, Tina?"

"No," she said firmly. "That part of me died with Bryant."

"But you're still impetuous."

Tina looked up with a frown. "No, not that, either."

"You came back here on a call from Kay."

Tina laughed. "If only you knew how many calls I've had from her over the years. No, this decision was well thought out and very calculated. I came back to earn the money to make my inn profitable."

"So that's why you signed with Generations—for purely pragmatic reasons."

Tina looked at him sharply. There was almost a trace of hurt in his voice, and she marveled at the ego of the man who could have thought that an interest in his product—or in him—prompted her to sign the Generations contract. "Exactly," she said. "As soon as the campaign is over, it's goodbye, Bettina, hello, Timberline. You knew that, Adam."

He shrugged, and she realized that he hadn't known, probably hadn't asked, the reasons for her return. "I only knew you were Bettina, headed for a comeback. But now that I know what you're up to, I'll have to do something to change your mind and keep you here longer. Something to develop that romantic side again," he said, and she lowered her eyes to avoid the look she knew was there.

"I'm afraid that won't be possible," Tina said, feigning interest in her coffee cup and only after a long pause looking up again to ask, "What about you, Adam? You've also been married...."

"And divorced—-several years ago. My ex-wife lives in Europe, and we communicate through lawyers. Not an unusual end to an American dream." His words had a bitter edge, and Tina thought suddenly of Holly and how difficult it must be for her, caught between warring parents. She remembered Holly mentioning the fight she'd had with her dad—a fight about her mother.

Tina asked Adam the question that she hadn't asked his daughter. "What about Holly? Does she see her mother often?"

Adam smiled coldly, and another look came into his eyes, turning them as hard as jet-black coal. "Not if I can help it." Then he pushed his chair back and extended his hand. "There's a wonderful pianist playing, I'm with the most beautiful woman in the city and I want to dance, not talk about my ex-wife. Indulge me."

Chapter 5

When they stepped onto the dance floor and Adam took her in his arms, Tina realized she'd made a big mistake. The sound of the piano was very faint, as if the keys were barely being tickled from far in the distance. A murmur of conversation drifted toward them, but it, like the sound of the piano, was distant, muffled. The dark oblong of the dance floor was lit only by an occasional flicker of light that reached it from candles on nearby tables. Secluded, they danced as if they were alone.

And alone was just what she didn't want to be, not with Adam Cole. He'd taken her hand and then hesitated, waiting for her. Too late to change her mind, she'd moved toward him, and although years had passed since she'd danced with a man, she stepped into his arms, thinking that perhaps men and women were born with the instinct to dance just as birds are born to fly and fish to swim, naturally. No, she cautioned herself against romanticism, recalling that dancing is learned early and comes back quickly, just like the ability to ride a bicycle.

However it happened, from early lessons or simple understanding, she was there, in his arms. His hand was warm and strong on the small of her back; she could feel the heat and strength through the cashmere. When her right hand slid innocently into his left, he grasped it firmly, possessively, and for a moment they remained still, two tall figures, alone like twin trees in a meadow, inches apart. Then he drew her closer until they touched—one part of their bodies after another blending.

Her face touched his, and she inhaled the crisp scent of his after-shave. He turned his head a little so that her forehead fit right above his ear in that little slope between eyebrow and cheekbone. It nestled there so perfectly that it seemed the spot had been made for her; she belonged there.

"Nice," he whispered softly against her ear, and Tina felt herself relax. That added to her undoing, for he enclosed her more completely in his arms so that his broad chest molded against her breasts, and his thighs whispered lightly against hers as he moved.

He was moving slowly, easily, over the dance floor with a steady rhythm that found the music but didn't try to overwhelm it, with a grace that captured a style but didn't misuse it. She wasn't just in his arms; she was moving with him as if they were two parts of the same being, meshed as one. Before that meshing was total and irrevocable, Tina tried to make some adjustment, to move away a little into two bodies again. But he held her firmly, and there was nothing she could do but give herself to the music, the night and Adam.

It was good, so good, Tina admitted, to be held in a man's arms and sway to the music of a dreamy piano. It brought back feelings almost forgotten or long hidden away. As the pianist drifted into a romantic old standard, Adam's hand moved slowly up her back, bringing her somehow even closer. Then he lowered his other hand—the one holding hers—until their clasped hands touched her leg, briefly but sensuously. Moments later he dropped her hand and wrapped her in both of his arms.

Tina knew exactly what he was doing. The champagne, the music, his arms around her, sliding seductively up and down the softness of her dress—all attested to his intentions. Adam was coming dangerously close to making love to her on the dance floor, and she was no longer doing anything to stop him. More than that, she was joining with him, clasping both of her arms around his neck and clinging to him, swaying with him, hips against hips, pelvis rubbing pelvis. In those places where their bodies pressed so erotically together, Tina felt a deep tingle of electricity. She tried to blame it on the champagne and the music, this feeling that now possessed her, but she knew it was more than that. The man who held her in his arms was a dangerous commodity, overbearing and arrogant and yet romantic, exciting and marvelously attractive.

The music stopped, but still he held her. Their lips were inches apart. He repeated a line from the song and asked, "Do you believe that, Tina? Do you believe the world smiles on lovers?" He was toying with her, teasing her while still not letting her leave the circle of his arms.

Tina took advantage of the moment to break the spell, moving a little away so she could look at him and respond, but without really answering his question. "I believe," she said, "that it's been a wonderful evening, but it's time to go home now."

No more than a split second passed before Adam's lips managed a smile. "Of course," he said. "It's getting late."

Their car was waiting for them, the driver leaning against the front fender dreamily smoking a cigarette. The smoke twisted above his head making a serpentine pattern in the still night air. When he saw them, he dropped the cigarette onto the street, put it out with the toe of his boot, adjusted his hat with a smile that was definitely meant for Tina and opened the door of the car.

Somehow, that series of actions, combined with the noise of the traffic still jamming the street even after midnight, brought back a sense of reality, and when Tina settled herself in the car, she managed to keep Adam at a strategic distance. He didn't try to move closer.

He gave the driver instructions and then settled back and looked at her with a smile that had none of the dance-floor magic in it; it was just a smile. Tina returned it, relieved.

They began to talk about the play, which they'd both enjoyed, and Tina felt that the evening would end with their being friends but no more; she could relax and look forward to working with Adam. But as they talked, he reached for her hand and held it. He didn't move any closer; he simply held her hand.

She'd been in the middle of a sentence when she felt his hand fitting over hers, and at first she hadn't been more than vaguely aware of it. But by the time she'd finished the sentence, Tina had the feeling that her words were nonsensical. She wasn't conscious of what she was saying, only of their hands clasped together.

If his touch wasn't as insinuating as his body when it molded to hers on the dance floor, it sparked her with the same force of electricity, causing a sort of panic. She tried to pull her hand away, but he held tightly.

"Don't," he said in a low voice that begged while it commanded. "Let me just hold your hand." It was such a simple request that she could find no reason to deny it, no reason except for the feelings that were stirring involuntarily inside of her. There'd been only a slight pause in their conversation, but even as it continued, she no longer had any idea what it was about. He'd begun to stroke her hand, his fingers moving thoughtfully up and down each finger as if memorizing the texture of her skin.

Tina hadn't wanted to sit close to him for fear that those sparks from the dance floor would flare up again. She'd succeeded in keeping her distance, but the touch of his powerful hand on hers had been enough to ignite her.

As he continued his explorative caresses, she gave up her attempt at conversation. She could hear their breathing in the quietness of the closed car. His seemed to come easily while hers was ragged, released in little gasps that corresponded with his touch. Never before had the touch of another's hand brought such accompanying shivers of delight; the taste of his lips on hers couldn't have been more thrilling. When Tina realized that, it just confused her more, especially now as his index finger began a new field of discovery, probing beneath the cuff of her sleeve, tracing a delicate blue vein with the tip of his finger.

She could feel her inhibitions dissolve under the sensual, rhythmic pressure of his fingers, and she cursed herself inwardly for the transparency of her emotions, at the same time letting herself imagine what those large and powerful hands would feel like on her hips, her thighs, her breasts.

Then as she struggled not to reveal those violently stirring emotions, Adam lifted her hand to his lips, kissing each finger lightly and then running his tongue along her palm, causing a little moan to escape from her throat.

Holding her hand against his face, he spoke to her again quietly. "You have strong hands," he said. "Soft but very strong."

Tina tried to grab the moment and remove the romance from it. "I . . . I do my share of hard work—at home in Colorado."

But the romance lingered as he nodded and kissed her hand once more, lips nibbling gently, tongue teasing, until she finally cried out, "No, Adam, please." That's when the car pulled up to the curb and the driver turned off the engine.

"We're home now, Tina," he said, and Tina looked around, surprised to see the driver get out of the car and open the door. She looked at Adam. He was smiling, and there was a twinkle in his eyes as if he knew exactly what kind of havoc his caresses had created on her nervous system, as if he realized that for most of the short drive across town, Tina hadn't been aware of where she was.

She knew now, and she managed to extract her hand from his at last, feeling only relief. She could breathe again. "Thanks, Adam," she said with finality, "for the wonderful evening. I'm glad we had this chance to..."

"Get to know each other better?" he teased.

"Yes," she returned with the glimmer of a smile, moving away so that the stream of light from the street lamp trickled between them, across his face, illuminating his features—the tanned skin, the white teeth, the thick dark hair and black, black eyes. Then he leaned toward her, and his face fell into the shadow again, but she could sense his lips near hers.

"I'll see you on Monday, then," she said suddenly before she slid across the leather seat to the door.

But Adam was following her, stepping out of the car onto the sidewalk and walking beside her into the foyer. He nodded to the doorman, and she realized with a start that Adam knew him. Of course, she remembered, he would be familiar with the building. Her apartment probably belonged to his company. Freeing herself from that thought and from him, Tina walked quickly down the hall.

In front of the door she paused, key in hand, and turned back toward him. "Thank you again, Adam," she said briskly. "It was a surprising evening, and I enjoyed it." She *had* enjoyed it—all of it. But now they were back to reality, standing in front of her apartment—his apartment—and she needed to make it perfectly clear that she wasn't one of his girls.

He must have guessed what was going through her mind, for he smiled, his eyes glittering, and she couldn't help thinking that he looked incredibly virile even in his dark suit and conservative tie. Tina extended her hand. "Thanks again," she said.

He took her hand but only to pull her toward him. "I want more than a handshake, Tina. Much more." His lips covered hers before she had a chance to respond, even to think.

Throughout the evening his lips had been dangerously close but never quite close enough for their breaths to mingle. Now, feeling their lips touching, Tina wondered why it had been so long in coming, this kiss that was warm and firm and tasted of champagne. She seemed to have been waiting all evening for it, and even as she made a halfhearted attempt to twist away, she didn't want it to end. It was a kiss so much more powerful than she'd expected, maybe because she'd gone so long without kisses or maybe just because it was Adam's kiss that she'd wanted madly, without admitting that want.

He pulled her closer, closer than he'd held her when they were dancing, locking them together so that their heartbeats, like their breaths, mingled and became one, pounding wildly. The touch of him, the taste—at last—caused her lips to open beneath his, and when his tongue slid inside her mouth, tracing the satin-smooth lining and skimming along the edge of her teeth, the desire made her limp. She seemed to feel him holding her up, keeping her from falling to the floor.

Then brazenly she returned the kiss, meeting tongue with tongue, letting a moan escape as she moved her mouth deliriously beneath his. Her blood was singing in her veins, pounding throughout her body, sending messages of the need that had first made her limp and now made her strong. Her breasts pushed against the buttons of his suit; her fingers dug into the back of his neck.

Adam tore his mouth from hers long enough to whisper, "I want you, Tina. I want you now, tonight." His voice was hoarse, rasping in her ear. Deep inside Tina felt a fluttering like that of a bird that had been long caged and now had to fly free.

She tried to answer, but his lips were on hers again, nibbling, licking, tasting, moving back and forth across her mouth and invading her with his determination. "Let me inside, Tina. Let me make love to you." His voice was compelling, his lips insistent, and her own body cried out for him.

But in the time that it took Adam to wrest the key from her hand and fumble for the lock, Tina's mind took control of her senses. Whatever happened that evening, she wasn't going to make love to Adam Cole. However much her body betrayed her, she wouldn't give herself to him. The reasons were jumbled, but they were there—many of them, and all rational. She didn't have to sort them out and enumerate them; that could happen later. She *knew*. This was wrong and she couldn't let it happen.

When the door swung open, Tina took the key and lifted her eyes to meet his. Her face was flushed, cheeks a bright red, lips swollen with his kisses. Her breath still came quickly and unevenly, and her heart was pounding so loudly that she was sure he could hear. But her gaze was steady, and so was her voice when she spoke.

"I'm sorry, Adam. I apologize for letting the evening get out of hand."

He shook his head slowly and moved toward her, but Tina put her hand on his arm to stop him. "The circumstances make this impossible."

"Tina, for God's sake," he said in that same husky voice that told her his emotions were still high, "what circumstances?"

"Our other involvement. It presents too many problems."

Tina knew that she was treading on shaky ground. Women seldom turned down Adam Cole, and those who did probably incurred his wrath. That was a chance she'd have to take; the wrath was to be preferred to the complications an involvement would present.

But she wasn't out of it yet; he still needed convincing. "This has nothing to do with business, Tina. Surely you understand that much."

"We might say so now—" she shook her head "—but I'm afraid I can see nothing but trouble ahead if we go any further. There're more reasons, though, many more that I can't sort out now and that I may never want to reveal, but please respect my feelings in this, Adam."

"Certainly," he said softly. "For now." He paused, his black eyes narrowed, the familiar look of arrogance back on his face. "But I'll remember," he said, "that nowhere in your excuse was there a hint that you didn't want me. You'll never convince me of that, Tina." He raised his hand and touched her face lightly, his dark eyes still intent on hers but without the romance in them now. Then he turned quickly and was gone.

Tina slipped inside the apartment and locked and bolted the door as if that action would protect her from Adam and the emotions associated with him during this admittedly wonderful but puzzling night.

He'd been right, of course. She did want him. The way he held her on the dance floor, his skillful touch on her hand in the car, his brazen kiss had made her remember how lonely she'd been, how long since a man had held her. And Adam was quite a man. But he could cause her pain; Tina's sense of loneliness told her that. She was vulnerable, a woman who could care deeply if roused by the right man, but a woman who could be just as deeply hurt.

Her strong sense of survival had warned Tina that making love to Adam would only result in trouble. She had listened, heeding that warning, and now she was glad, even though the need was still there, unquenched. To quench it would be a mistake. He was a man to whom women were ornaments, and after a night in bed with her, he would have shown up on the set without even the memory of what had happened, while she would have been shaken, used.

Tina stripped off her dress, hung it in the closet and stood in the middle of the room in her slip. The material, a soft, clinging satin, seemed somehow rough against her skin, which still remembered his touch and ached for it. She couldn't ignore the excitement she'd felt in his arms and still felt along the surface of her skin. It had surprised her, that reaction.

But she'd simply been manipulated, Tina tried to tell herself, hugging her arms across her breasts and not being able to forget. He'd manipulated her first to the theater, then to dinner and then into his arms. Slick, smooth, a real operator, he was also her client, her boss, and no matter her feelings, no matter her years of loneliness, she was here to do a job, take her money and run—and not get involved with her employer. There was enough tension and anxiety associated with Generations without adding an involvement with the man in charge.

Tina took off her slip, trying to ignore the need pounding through her naked body, slipped into a gown and began to brush her hair, still sure that she'd made the right decision. One Cole in her life was quite enough. She and Holly had to work together every day, and there was no room for Adam except at a distance.

A week later Tina was standing beside Holly on the top floor of an unfinished skyscraper. The foundation and concrete sides of the building were in place as well as some of the lower floors, but not the one they were balanced on. There, only rows of steel beams separated them from the level twenty feet below. Tina had no idea how permission had ever been wrangled from the builders and the city for them to ride the makeshift elevator up to the top of nowhere.

The wind was blowing as they huddled together near an unfinished wall that stood at the corner of the building. Beyond it—nothing but air. Tina didn't look down and neither, she noticed, did Holly as they responded unhesitatingly to the director's commands, just so they could get back on the shaky elevator and return to solid ground.

Everything would have been over quickly except for the man cast as a burly construction worker. His role was to walk past them carrying a load of two-by-four boards on his shoulder and then turn, notice Tina and Holly and shrug as if there were nothing unusual about two beautiful women standing precariously atop an unfinished building.

But not one move the man made in take after take seemed to satisfy Adam Cole. Tina had the feeling he would have preferred to play the part himself, but failing that, Adam stood at the director's elbow, watching while the poor actor completed his action again and again, and Tina and Holly struggled to look fresh and—more difficult—unafraid. The wind whipped around them. Holly whispered that she could feel the building swaying, and Tina definitely felt her stomach churning. David, who'd already gotten the still shots he wanted, sat on the edge of an unsupported beam, swinging his legs above the chasm, which only added to their nervousness. But pros both, they kept on smiling until, on the nineteenth take, both the director and Adam were satisfied.

Tina and Holly rushed for the little three-passenger elevator, getting there first and then having to wait for someone to close the heavy steel gate after them. "I'll do that," Adam said as he got into the elevator. Tina hadn't been this close to him since that night a week before, but he'd been watching her, eyes narrowed against the glare, during every take. Now, squeezed into the small space with them, he told Holly that she'd done a good job, nodded to Tina and commented that he hoped the effect he wanted had been achieved.

"This location was my idea," he said, not surprising Tina in the least. "Something about being on the edge of a skyscraper in a situation that could be made to look dangerous appealed to me."

"*Made* to look dangerous?" Holly repeated. "I was scared to death."

"Well, of course no one was in the slightest danger at any time," Adam explained to his daughter, "I made sure that every precaution was taken. You walked and stood only on secured areas. Frankly, my only concern was that David stopped shooting so soon, but of course no one can tell him anything. I hope he achieved the effect I wanted."

"I'm sure he did," Tina found herself saying.

Adam looked at her sharply. "Well, we won't know until we see his proofs. But his stills will have to correspond perfectly with the scenes we use from the film in order to carry out the theme."

Both Tina and Holly had shot for television and print simultaneously in the past, but Adam seemed intent upon explaining his procedure, so they listened. What else could they do, Tina thought, pressed together in a small elevator high in an unfinished skyscraper.

There was something about his authoritative manner, his challenging look, his knowing voice that reminded Tina of the man she'd met at her test, but not the one she'd been out with just days before. This man didn't appeal to her at all. Maybe that's what he hoped for, she thought; maybe this was his way of telling her that she'd had her chance and it was all professionalism from now on. If so, Tina was relieved. The pressure was off.

"I think you'll be pleased with the results," Tina ventured. "Holly and I work well together."

Adam raised an eyebrow. "Are you always so sure of yourself?" he asked as the elevator reached the ground floor. Then, without waiting for Tina's response, he stepped off and pulled back the gate.

"Take a break, gals, while we get this shot set up," one of the advance crew called out as Adam walked away from them without another word.

Tina and Holly headed for the canvas chairs that had been set up in one corner of the construction site. "Boy, is Dad in a mood today," Holly said as she flopped into a chair. "Glad all that flak wasn't directed at me."

Tina hesitated before she spoke, realizing her relationship with Holly was important, the beginning of a friendship that, however tenuous, was just getting off the ground. She wondered whether she should remain silent but quickly decided to be honest with the girl, at least to a point. "I think he's upset with me," she said. "We went out last week—on business—and had a slight disagreement."

"I knew you were out together. You were all over the papers, but as for the rest—" Holly barely suppressed a giggle. "Oh, m'god," she said, "do you mean Dad made a pass and you said no?" Without waiting for confirmation, she added, "That's probably a first. You realize he has millions of women wild over him."

Tina nodded, looking at Holly quizzically. "Doesn't that bother you? All the women in his life?"

Holly shook her head. "It would if I thought there was a chance for him and Mom to get back together, but that's out of the question. Hopeless. They really hate each other." She slung one long leg over the arm of the director's chair.

"I'm sorry," Tina said, wincing at the girl's honesty but aware that her own words sounded hollow and meaningless. "I know it's tough," she added lamely.

Holly shrugged. "So what else is new?" She reached into her tote bag and pulled out a pack of cigarettes, offering one to Tina, who shook her head. Holly put a gold-tipped cigarette between her red lips and lit it.

"I didn't know you smoked," Tina said, trying to put some disapproval in her voice without actually nagging.

"Only now and then when I feel in the mood—and Dad's not around. Anyway, about all the women he sees, it's kind of like a revolving door. One this week, one the next." Holly inhaled deeply and then went into a fit of coughing.

"That's really not good for you," Tina offered.

"I know," Holly said, tossing the cigarette onto the dirt floor. "What I'm trying to say about Dad's social life is that I don't take any of it too seriously."

"I guess I figured that out," Tina said slowly, for she *had* figured it out, and she was more glad than before that she hadn't let herself become a part of the long procession of women in and out the door of Adam's life. She couldn't help wondering if his penchant for beautiful women—and lots of them—had been the cause of the marital breakup or if it had been, as Kay suggested, dedication to his work. Adam seemed capable of living in both worlds, and Tina doubted if she'd ever find the answers. Holly wasn't likely to share with her, and she and Adam certainly weren't destined for any more intimate evenings together, not after what happened—or didn't happen—between them last week.

Bill Fontana stepped through the gaping hole that was the doorway and called out to them. "Okay, girls, we're set up outside the building. Come on—we've still

got a page of the storyboard to shoot before we lose
the sun."

"Mrs. Harris, may I see you after class?"

Tina looked up nervously from her desk at Dr.
Stuart Forrester and nodded her acquiescence. The
rest of the students gathered up books, jackets, brief-
cases and handbags and straggled out of the room except for an older man, who quickly made his way to
the professor's desk to beat Tina out of first place. She
didn't care; in fact, she was relieved. Whatever Dr.
Forrester had to say to her, she couldn't imagine it
would be complimentary. Her participation in the
class had hardly been significant.

She waited patiently while the gray-haired man
asked a complicated question about a poem they'd
read that night. Tina didn't even understand the
question, much less the professor's answer. Apparently there was more to the poem than she'd realized.

As Dr. Forrester continued his explanation, Tina
was aware that she'd stopped listening and was
watching him intently. He wasn't at all what she'd
expected when she signed up for the course, envision-
ing a middle-aged man, tweedy and pipe-smoking. Dr.
Forrester was young, possibly a few years younger
than Tina, very slender, his light brown hair flecked
with gold. He did wear glasses and in that way at least
was professorial. His eyes behind the tortoiseshell rims
were blue and friendly.

The other student, finally satisfied with Dr. Forrester's response, picked up his armful of books and with
a perfunctory nod at Tina left the classroom. The
professor's appraising blue eyes turn toward her. "Did
you hear any of that discussion?" he asked.

"Bits and pieces," Tina responded, not about to admit that she'd been surprised by the heavy thoughts associated with the poem.

"Well, it was all hogwash, believe me," came the response. "When a student is hell-bent on pontificating, sometimes it's just best to let him have his way."

Tina smiled happily, relieved that her interpretation hadn't been so far off.

"We tend to overdo depth of meaning sometimes, don't you think?"

Tina, who hadn't been encouraged—in the past week under Adam Cole's thumb—to think at all, was happy to agree.

"Now, about your choice of poet for the class paper—" he picked up a list from his desk and glanced down at it "—I see you've decided on Emily Brontë."

Tina breathed a sigh of relief. Apparently this little conference was only to discuss her paper. Still uncertain in the academic world, she'd imagined all sorts of wrongs she'd committed. But she should have known better. Mrs. Harris, the woman who sat in the back of the room quietly taking notes and listening to everything that was said without comment, hadn't ventured far enough into academia to go wrong. Unless, she thought, choosing Emily Brontë was, somehow, a mistake.

"I'd read her novels," Tina explained, "but I had no idea she also wrote poetry. I thought it might be interesting to see if the same themes were carried through the prose and the poetry." She spoke quickly, not sure how much he wanted of what she suspected were inanities.

He removed his glasses and smiled at her. "It's a very good choice, an interesting one, which none other of my students thought of. They've all gone for the old standbys—Keats, Shelley, Browning.'' He nodded. ''Yes, I like the choice. It shows an original mind.''

''Thank you.'' Tina smiled up at him, feeling like a child who'd been rewarded with a special treat—as well she should, she thought, having had little in the way of compliments recently for anything other than her looks. And those had been grudging, at least when given by Adam Cole.

Stuart Forrester stood beside his desk looking down at her for a long moment, smiling awkwardly, endearing himself to Tina without knowing it before he spoke again. ''I have a book on the Brontës you might want to borrow. It's not available in the library stacks.''

''I'd appreciate that,'' Tina said. She didn't add that since joining the class she hadn't begun her research, finding time only to read her assignments between fittings, makeup and travel to the remote shooting sites Adam Cole managed to come up with.

''The book will be a great help, I'm sure.'' He picked up his corduroy jacket from the back of a chair and walked to the door, pausing a moment to wait for her before he flicked off the light. He didn't dress like a professor, either, Tina observed, but wore jeans, Top-Siders, a pale blue cotton shirt and no tie. He was lanky and just barely as tall as Tina.

''My office is upstairs. We're overflowing at the school, and some of us have been relegated to these old buildings at the edge of the square.'' He smiled, letting her precede him up the stairs. ''Actually, I like it over here; it's a little more remote and peaceful.''

He ushered Tina into the office with a wave of his hand. Books and papers were piled on tables, chairs and the floor and teetered precariously on the windowsill. There was a pleasant air of disarray, a kind of careless disregard for order that somehow put Tina at ease. Dr. Forrester rummaged through a stack of books, tossing questions over his shoulder as he searched for the elusive Brontë volume. "You're not from New York, are you, Mrs. Harris?"

"No, from Colorado. I moved here in September." Tina had no intention of revealing her profession and ruining what little respect she'd built up with her teacher.

"Your husband was transferred, I guess." The comment was casual and natural.

"No, my husband died several years ago," Tina answered. "I moved here alone."

The professor located the book and stood with it in his hand, an embarrassed expression on his face. "I'm sorry to hear that. About your husband, I mean, not that you're in New York." He looked terribly ill at ease, and Tina observed that she'd never met a man so genuinely shy, outside the comfort of his classroom. "Here's the book," he said, thrusting it toward her.

Tina put the book in her bag. "I promise to take good care of it."

"I'm sure you will. Maybe we can discuss it sometime over coffee—before you turn in the paper. Emily Brontë was a complex woman—like the rest of her unusual family."

"Yes." Tina was happy to be able to agree. "I recall that from the introduction to *Wuthering Heights*."

The professor, pleased, nodded in agreement. An awkward silence followed, but Tina quickly filled it by thanking him again before she turned to leave. "I'll

see you in class on Tuesday, Dr. Forrester,'' she added
as she opened the door.

"Yes," he agreed, calling after her. "And it's
Stuart, please—at least outside the classroom," he
added with a grin that Tina missed.

She walked along Washington Square toward University Avenue, mingling with other students and
feeling just like one of them. It was a beautiful October night, crisp and breezy with a full moon sailing
across the sky. She felt very content that she was doing
something on her own, without help from Bettina. She
looked nothing like the glamorous image that David
and the others strove to capture each day, with her hair
hanging loose, wearing a bulky sweater and slacks.
She was just Tina. And Dr. Forrester was Stuart—at
least out of class. She smiled to herself, thinking about
his kindness. She liked him, Tina decided. If all professors were like Stuart, then college was going to be
a pleasure.

She passed a little café crowded with students and
decided to go in for a cup of coffee. Sitting at the table surrounded by the conversation of a college community, Tina felt as though she belonged. Stuart had
been pleased with her comments and her choice for a
paper—and interested in her for herself, as no man
had ever been except Bryant.... Tina smiled. Ever
since she'd begun the course in English poetry, she'd
been nagged by the thought that there was something
familiar about Stuart Forrester, something that attracted her. She sipped her coffee and smiled as it came
to her. He reminded her of Bryant.

Chapter 6

They were shooting inserts in the studio, picking up scenes from the the rooftop commercial, when the messenger appeared carrying a large package. He'd ignored the flashing red light and walked right into the set.

"Somebody needs to sign for this," he called out.

The camera kept rolling, and the director didn't look around, Tina continued her action, reaching into the frame for a Generations jar.

"Somebody..." the bored messenger called out.

"Is that from Stern Studios?" Adam asked.

"Yeah," came the response. "Stern. West Thirty-eighth. For Adam Cole. You Cole?"

Adam nodded and got up to sign for the package. Bill Fontana joined him as Tina ended her action on the set and the director gave her the order to cut. "That's the last insert, Adam," he said, glancing at the storyboard the script girl was holding. "You satisfied?"

"I'm satisfied," Adam said. He'd opened the package, and he and Bill were looking through its contents, which Tina knew were David's stills from the commercial. She also knew that Adam had been nervously awaiting them all day. Adam hadn't yet learned what Tina had known for years: David never missed.

"Is there a light board around here?" Adam asked.

"In the back office," the director responded, adding to Tina and the crew, "That's a wrap."

As Adam and Bill headed down the hall, Adam called out over his shoulder, "Don't leave, Tina. I want to see you."

Tina collapsed into one of the canvas chairs as the crew began to strike the set. She was still sitting there half an hour later when Bill Fontana came out of the office, picked up his jacket and headed for the door.

"Good Lord," he said when he saw Tina. "Are you still here?" The crew had finished dismantling the set and were stacking lights against the wall.

"He told me to wait, so I'm waiting." Several times Tina had been tempted to get up and leave but had decided that Adam was in no mood for insubordination.

"Maybe he wants you to see the transparencies," Bill offered.

"I can't imagine why." She wanted to see them, but she knew full well that models, who were usually the focal point, often didn't see their work until the final ad and then only when they came across it in a magazine. "I'm the model," she added for Bill's edification, "not the ad manager."

Bill smiled and touched her shoulder. "Sometimes, with this guy, roles get shifted. Adam!" he called out toward the open door at the back of the studio. "Tina's still here."

"Tell her to wait. I'll be with her in a minute," came the response.

Bill shrugged and put on his jacket. "'Ours is not to reason why...'" he said as he gave Tina a wave and disappeared through the steel doors into the street.

In the back office of the production studio, Adam sat on a swivel chair in front of a light board that was lined with color transparencies. There was no reason for him to keep Tina waiting—except the demands of his ego. Adam admitted that much to himself. He was used to having what he wanted—and whom he wanted. Tina had turned him down, setting off a complex series of emotions within him. Now, over a week later, he still hadn't been able to work them all out. He was certain of only one thing: he needed to get the upper hand in their relationship again.

He'd tried to recapture it during the rooftop filming, but he'd come off looking petulant and angry, a fact his daughter had pointed out to him later. Now he'd achieved his purpose in the most mundane way—making Tina, who obviously was tired from the day's work, wait for no reason.

Yet there was a reason. He wanted to share the shots with her. He studied them again carefully, admitting as he had admitted to Bill that he was pleased with David's work despite the man's refusal to listen to him. Tina and Holly looked natural together, both suitably aloof and blasé, not even deigning to notice the approval of the construction worker or the danger of their precarious perch.

Adam and Bill had agreed on the two shots to be enlarged, and he was curious to know what Tina thought. This was a first; never had Adam Cole asked the opinion of his models, not even his daughter, and yet he wanted Tina's opinion. Still, he kept her waiting.

Adam had circled the best shots with a grease pencil. They were obvious choices, but he decided to erase the orange marks and see which she chose. That might be interesting.

Finally he stood up and went to the door. "Tina," he called to the lone figure sitting in the director's chair under a bare overhead bulb in the empty studio. When he called her, she looked up, and Adam thought for a moment that he'd never seen a more beautiful woman. And he'd seen plenty of beautiful women in his time. He caught his breath, paused a beat and then said in a voice he hoped was even, "Would you mind coming back here for a moment?"

Tina kept her response to herself as she got up and walked down the hall. She certainly *would* mind, just as she'd minded sitting for a half hour in a bare studio when she was tired from a long day's work and wanted to go home. But she'd been chosen to do Adam's bidding today, whatever the perverse reason.

She entered the office to find him leaning against a long table, his arms folded across his chest, one leg crossed over the other. His tie was loosened, and his sleeves were rolled up to display Adam Cole at his most casual. She tried to mirror his relaxed demeanor, but somewhere deep inside was the feeling that another confrontation was on the way.

"Thanks for waiting," he said.

Tina's lips curved in the semblance of a smile. She could have ignored his request and left the studio with the rest of the union workers, refusing to stay one minute past her contracted day's work, but she'd stayed, and she wouldn't even complain to the union. From the beginning she'd tried to heed Kay's admonishment to behave herself and to do whatever Adam Cole requested—within reason. He was the boss, from a professional point of view, and obviously this was a professional call—asking her to look at the transparencies—and not a personal one.

He flicked a switch under the light board. "I thought you might like to see the results of the skyscraper shoot." In his tone was the feeling that he was doing her a favor and not, as was the case, that he'd wanted to share the pictures with her. "The concept worked out well. I saw the rushes from the commercial yesterday, and these stills picked up all the best scenes and all the right angles."

She hadn't moved from the doorway. Adam rearranged the sheets on the board. It was an unnecessary action, but as he completed it he was able to get a glimpse of Tina in profile. He realized that she'd taken off her camera makeup. What he saw was a woman far removed from the earlier haute-couture image. She'd pulled her hair back with a scarf and looked casual, even fresh, after a long day's work. Sitting under the light in the studio there'd been a glow about her; here, closer and under more brutal light, she still glowed. A tightening in his throat and a quickening below his rib cage told Adam what he already knew—he still wanted her.

He finished arranging the sheets and was left with nothing else to do and, uncharacteristically, nothing to say. He cleared his throat and turned to her. "Why don't you come over and have a look?" he asked.

She crossed the room in a swirl of movement, graceful, even under the trench coat she'd belted around her long lithe body. Her eyes ran quickly over the pictures.

"What do you think?" he asked after a moment, wondering if she'd noticed the husky tone of his voice.

Tina glanced up at him, her eyes cool. "I think they're great...just as I predicted." She couldn't keep the self-congratulatory inflection from her voice.

Adam raised one eyebrow and smiled. She wasn't giving an inch. Not about to be intimidated, she was still as sure of herself as she'd been since they first chose her for the job.

"The camera is David's; the face is yours; but you will agree, won't you, that the idea wasn't so bad after all?"

Tina nodded her head. "Yes," she answered. "I wasn't thrilled about being on top of that building, but the concept worked. Your concept," she added.

"Exactly. I'm glad there's something we finally agree on." His dark eyes bit into hers, but Tina's never wavered. She knew exactly what message Adam was sending her in that look, and she was determined not to flinch under it.

"Bill and I have agreed on the two best shots. We'll enlarge them and then decide on the one for the ad. Just out of curiosity," he said, wanting to make it clear that her opinion was of little value, "I'd like to know your choice."

Tina bent over and looked more carefully at the sheets, moving them around, eliminating and narrowing down quickly. Then she picked up one sheet.

"Numbers twenty-three and twenty-four," she said without hesitation.

Adam smiled. "Interesting."

Tina straightened up and looked across at him. She was still wearing the very high heels from the afternoon shoot, and her eyes were almost on a level with his. "My choices are the same as yours?" When he nodded, she added quickly, "I was in the business for a long time, Adam, and I learned over the years how to give the camera just what it wanted. All of these shots are good because we're all pros—David, you and me—and Holly, of course. But these are the best. They're just what you were after."

There was the confidence again, Adam thought, and it was certainly justified. Once more, he'd lost the upper hand gained by keeping her waiting. "And which one of these two?" he asked.

"The first one, number twenty-three," she responded immediately.

He picked up a loupe from the desk and handed it to her. "Look closely, and I think you'll see why that's the wrong choice."

Tina held the loupe to the frame and looked at it as Adam spoke. "David always brackets his shots, as you know. What you see there, in numbers twenty-three and twenty-four, is virtually the same shot with a little more light in twenty-four. Just enough to wash out the problems."

"What problems?" Tina asked, looking more carefully. She actually had no idea what he was getting at. The first shot was sharper with more contrast, nearly perfect.

"Forget the worker and Holly and concentrate on your face." As Tina held the loupe to the transparency, Adam said, "You're a beautiful woman, obviously, but the aging is beginning to show—in the slight puffiness around your lids, the little lines at the corners of your eyes, the crease—"

Tina put down the magnifying glass and stood up to face him, somehow finding more than her full height and meeting his eyes directly. "I know my own face, Adam, as well as anyone."

"Of course you do." His tone was conciliatory. "I was only explaining my decision against this shot. I'm sure you'll agree when you see them blown up. There'll always be an alternative as long as David is photographing this campaign. But for the future, I was thinking that many women your age undergo cosmetic surgery. A slight tightening of the lids—"

Before he finished the sentence, Adam caught a glimpse of Tina's face and realized that he'd overstepped his bounds. He didn't even know why he'd brought the subject up except that, once more, he'd managed to lose the upper hand and wanted to get it back at any cost.

Tina's jaw was set in a hard line, and her eyes shot tiny blazes of blue fire. "You called me back here to suggest I have plastic surgery?" She spoke as if she couldn't believe what she'd heard.

Whatever had dictated his words, Adam was defensive now and not about to back down. "Many models find surgery helpful. It can extend a career for years and years. I'm not suggesting your whole face needs to be remodeled, Tina, only—"

Tina moved away from Adam and his words, back to her earlier position by the door. "I'm not interested in extending my career, Adam. It will end the day that this campaign is over—if not before," she added boldly.

He stood glaring across the desk at her. "I think you're overreacting, Tina," he said stonily.

"And I think you presume too much. Interfering in my personal life goes beyond the bounds of business." She tried to keep her voice cool, tried to keep the anger under control. But even to her own ears her words came out tense and tight.

If Adam was angry, it didn't show in his voice, which was soft and low. And perhaps deadly, Tina decided. "Anything concerning you is the business of Century Cosmetics—and my business," he responded.

"Then if you really care about your cosmetic company and Generations, you'll think a little more realistically about this campaign. If you remember, you were searching for a real woman for Generations, a woman 'exulting in her maturity,'" she mimicked. "Well, Adam, in case you haven't noticed lately, this is what a real woman looks like." She threw back her shoulders and lifted her chin, showing him a profile which, if he had let himself admit it, once more took his breath away.

But Tina didn't know that; she knew only his words, not his thoughts. "This is the face I've grown up with," she said, "and every line on it has been earned through pain and laughter and love." She was glad she'd removed all the camera makeup, glad for the pitiless overhead light. "I'm damned if I'll change it for a stupid advertising whim—even if it's the whim of the president of Century Cosmetics."

"Tina—" he tried to interrupt.

She wasn't about to listen. "If you want a twenty-year-old, Adam, then by all means get one, with my blessing." Tina retrieved her bag from the desk and opened the office door. As she turned to leave she looked back over her shoulder.

"Oh, just out of curiosity," she said, mocking him again, "which shot did Bill Fontana choose?"

"Number twenty-three," she heard him say as she made her exit triumphantly, sweeping her trench coat up around her and closing the door with more force than was necessary. It was an exit worthy of every Grade B movie she'd ever seen.

Adam, too, had noticed the similarity to a bad movie in their whole scene, but her melodramatic departure had carried it a little too far, he decided. He'd been a fool to mention aging. He'd done it without thinking, in a sort of futile gesture to reestablish his authority. That had been a mistake, but damn the woman for reacting so violently. What he'd said was true, whether or not it needed to be said.

Adam flicked off the light board and picked up his coat. The scene had escalated so quickly between them that he'd hardly realized what was happening. After his initial comment about plastic surgery, he should have let the topic drop.

Hell, he'd known Tina was impetuous; in fact, she was far too impetuous to be completely trusted and had to be handled carefully. Now he'd lost for good what control he ever had. It was fourth down in this relationship, and he had long yardage to go. He wasn't even on the scoreboard, and Adam Cole had run out of plays.

For a moment he wrestled with an outlandish thought: he could fire her. Then, shaking his head, he put it away, but not without a moment of real contentment as he imagined the look on her face when they informed her she was no longer the Generations Woman.

After two long blocks across town, taken at breakneck pace, Tina finally slowed down and caught her breath. The ending of that long scene had been all wrong. As soon as she'd heard the door slam behind her, Tina knew that she'd overreacted. She should have kept her cool under the force of his remarks, but she'd never been able to take Adam Cole lightly. She cursed him for causing all the wrong reactions in her.

Her rational mind tried to get a hold on her emotions, arguing that it wasn't at all unusual for women in her profession to have minor cosmetic surgery to extend their years in the field and therefore their earnings. It certainly wasn't unheard of for an agent or even a client to make such a suggestion to a model. In a business where women were the personification of the product, it was natural that everyone have a stake in the success or failure of that symbol.

Tina hated it. She'd hated it before, and she was still rankled by being looked at as a commodity, not as a person. Adam Cole had dredged up in one afternoon all the anger she'd kept suppressed over the years. And more than that, he'd done it with arrogance and condescension. There'd been no reason for his remarks, since he'd admitted himself that she was still right for his campaign. Then why had he brought up her age at all, if not to prove his authority? Or to give her pain? Well, maybe he'd shown the authority, but he hadn't caused her pain, only anger. Tina was proud of every line on her face, particularly when she knew that once this campaign was over no camera or client would have to fret about the lines again.

As she charged along Fifty-ninth Street, her mind played a rondelet in rhythm to her pounding feet, enumerating those women before her who had been spared her indignities. No one had asked Emily Brontë to have her eyes fixed, or Eleanor Roosevelt or even Gloria Steinem. Her mind went over a litany of women known for what they were, not how they looked. She even threw in a miscellaneous paean to Stuart Forrester, who cared nothing for her beauty. Then Tina realized the difference between herself and those women she admired. She was a model whose face was her fortune. But not for long, she swore; not for long.

By the time she reached her apartment building, Tina's anger had refocused. She remembered who was responsible for her indignation. Adam Cole had kept her waiting as long as he chose and then called her in to humiliate her. It didn't take a genius to discern his motivation. She turned him down the night of the opening, and he wanted to get even by lording his power over her. It was a pure and simple case of resurgence of the male ego, and Adam certainly had an excess of that commodity.

Tina searched in her bag for the mailbox key, her thoughts still darkly on her employer, wondering, spitefully, what would happen if she left, just picked up and walked off. That's what he deserved. She wrenched her mail from the confines of the box. What she'd give, Tina thought, her lips curving wickedly, to see his face when they gave him the news that his star model had disappeared.

Tina paused at the table in her foyer and turned on the light, which sparkled through the glass chandelier. She'd been fond of this little entrance hall with its Queen Anne table and Aubusson rug until she realized that everything in it—and in the rest of the elegantly furnished apartment—belonged, if not personally to Adam, to his company. She put the mail on the table and sorted through the flyers and bills looking for a letter from Kam and Eli but finding nothing. She hadn't heard from them since sending the last check, which meant all was going well—or nothing was going well. She thought of calling and decided to take a bath first, relax and have a good long drink of brandy. Then she'd be better able to face the latest disaster at the inn—the failed dishwasher, broken van, cracked plumbing—or worse. It was the ''worse'' that really bothered her—a catastrophe of unmendable dimensions. She shook the thought away. Right now she couldn't deal with any more problems, large or small.

Two hours later Tina felt light-years improved. She'd heated soup for her dinner, let a hot bath soak the tension from her back and shoulders and then curled up in her old terry-cloth bathrobe in front of the fire, deep into the book Stuart Forrester had given her. A lined pad lay on the table beside her, and every now and then Tina stopped to make a note about an idea or fact that especially intrigued her. She hadn't been a student for many years, and getting back into the groove was proving to be fun. She was excited about the prospect of hard work that would allow her to use her mind and not her smile to prove herself. Delving into the book on her lap was an adventure that far surpassed standing on the edge of an unfinished building posing for David's camera—and Adam Cole's ego.

When the buzzer rang, Tina was so deeply into nineteenth-century Yorkshire that it took a moment to orient herself. Without thinking, her mind still on the tangled lives of the Brontës, she padded barefoot across the pale rose carpet to the hall and buzzed her visitor into the building. It was almost nine o'clock, and she imagined that Kay was stopping by for a drink after an evening at Bloomingdale's. By now Kay was well-known to the doorman.

But there was someone else equally well-known to him. The voice that accompanied the knock on her apartment door brought Tina fully back to reality.

"Tina, it's Adam. Open the door so I can talk to you. It's important."

This was the second time in one day that she was being presented with a demand from her employer. She looked down at her worn terry robe and bare feet. She'd washed her hair, and it hung, still damp, around a face totally devoid of makeup. Well, why not let him in, she thought, and really give him something to criticize? Not hesitating, Tina pulled open the door.

She was greeted by a profusion of flowers. They spilled out of Adam's arms onto the floor, bunches of delightfully scented color—roses, red and yellow, and sprays of spring blossoms forced open in a greenhouse and flown to New York to be purchased at great expense. Hidden behind the masses of flowers, his face was suitably apologetic.

"Actually, I've never been very good at apologies," he said. "In fact, this might be a first for me." He began to divest himself of some of the bouquets, pressing them haphazardly into Tina's arms. "I didn't know what kind you liked so I bought some of everything—except orchids. I had the idea you wouldn't like orchids."

Tina took half a step backward, put the flowers he'd given her on the table and was immediately handed more. Adam seemed almost boyish in his enthusiasm, not at all like the hard, cold man she'd clashed with earlier in the day. This different Adam was gentler, less decisive and very compelling.

Tina tried to harden her heart to match the steeliness of her words. "This is very nice, Adam. Very generous but hardly necessary."

"Oh, but it is necessary," he disagreed, "to help me admit that I was wrong. You're great the way you are, Tina. That's what Generations is all about. I was out of line today, and I'd like to explain—"

"Oh, I think I understand perfectly." Tina peered over the mass of fragrant blossoms that she cradled in her arms. Their scent was provocative, exciting and almost overpowering. She added them to the pile on the table.

"You could invite me in, Tina. I'm not dangerous."

Somehow, Tina knew better, but it was too late. When she turned toward the table, he'd taken another step over the threshold and was making his way inside.

"We need to talk," he insisted, "and we also need to get all those flowers in water." Another step and he was able to close the door behind him, now firmly established in her territory.

She hesitated and then shrugged. "The kitchen's this way," she said before she realized that he knew damn well where the kitchen—and every other room—

was located. He made no comment but followed after her.

Between them, they managed to find every vase, bowl, pitcher and jar that the apartment had to offer. As they stuffed roses, lilies, peonies, chrysanthemums and a dozen other flowers Tina couldn't name into the containers, she began to chuckle. "Looks like someone died." She'd struggled to hold on to her anger, but it had disappeared under the weight of Adam's floral onslaught.

"I guess it is a little overpowering," Adam agreed, brushing sprigs of florist greenery from his suit. "I tend to get carried away, but at least this gets my message across."

"Message?" Tina asked warily.

"Just what I said in the hall, Tina. You *are* the Generations Woman." That he'd ever considered firing her seemed preposterous, Adam realized.

"Even with my wrinkles?" There was neither laughter nor teasing in her tone.

"You're not going to let me forget that, are you?"

Tina forced a final stem into an arrangement and looked up at him. "Never." But neither would she leave the campaign, Tina realized.

Adam smiled, a real smile that creased his cheeks and lit his eyes. His words were more unexpected than the smile. "You keep me honest, Tina, and I like that. We should get the enlargements tomorrow, and I have a feeling that when I've seen them I'll agree with Bill— and you. Hell, I'm trying to appeal to the mature woman, and I can't do that with photographs of someone who looks like a schoolgirl."

Tina laughed. "Well, I doubt if you could find any shots where I looked quite that young."

"I'm afraid that's what I was trying to do. Holly's the kid in this campaign—and you're the woman. I won't forget it again. I was trying to control you, Tina, to show you who's boss. I was wrong, and I'm sorry."

Tina stood beside him surrounded by a myriad of flowers that had turned the tiny kitchen into a fragrant hothouse, amazed to hear Adam's words. Not only had he apologized extravagantly, he'd admitted that she might be right.

"Am I forgiven?" he persisted, scooping up a few flowers that had fallen to the floor and poking them randomly into vases, avoiding her gaze.

Tina's answer came thoughtfully. "I should also apologize, for lack of professionalism. I've been in this business long enough to know your remarks weren't meant personally, Adam. But I still have a difficult time being viewed as a commodity to be packaged and sold. It bothered me before; it still does."

He shook his head. "Believe me, Tina, I don't see it that way. If I get out of line again, you have my permission to shoot me down."

Tina's mind was working furiously, trying to understand what had happened here in this flower-filled kitchen. Obviously her performance at the studio had caused him more concern than she'd imagined. Obviously he wanted her forgiveness. She wasn't quite sure whether he wanted to be forgiven as a man who'd made a mistake or as a client who couldn't afford to lose his prize package. Either way, they'd both been right—and both wrong. She accepted the apology.

"Truce," she said, her tone degrees more friendly.

He grinned at her, a charming, tension-lowering smile that made him seem years younger and terribly approachable. "Then we can celebrate. I'd like to take you to dinner."

He'd looked at her then—and earlier, since she'd opened the door to him—as if she were wearing not a worn robe but a Givenchy gown. Under his gaze she'd forgotten to feel discomfort or embarrassment.

"I've already had dinner—a bowl of soup," she explained, and when there was no response, offered her own invitation. "I could fix you some soup, a salad..."

"Thanks, I'd like that very much," came the unexpected answer.

Feeling her sense of unreality increase by the moment, Tina turned on the stove to heat the pot of soup while Adam looked in the cabinet and came up with a bowl. Unreal or not, there was a familiarity about the scene that prevented Tina from even considering changing her clothes to put on something more appropriate to the image of Bettina. The pressure was off her. Tina decided to enjoy the evening, whatever it was all about.

Adam held out the bowl as she spooned in the vegetable soup. "Let's sit in front of your fire and talk, Tina. I'd like for you to give me another chance to prove that I'm not such a bad guy after all, maybe just a little intense some of the time." He opened the drawer and reached for a spoon. "That is, if you're not doing something else. I didn't even think that I might be interrupting—"

"No, I was just reading," Tina responded, realizing for the first time that she'd completely forgotten about the Brontës.

It didn't take long for the air of unreality to subside into a kind of hominess. Adam had finished his soup and a salad they'd thrown together from what they could find in the refrigerator and taken the dishes to the kitchen. When he returned to the living room, he sat down on the sofa. It was large and comfortable, slipcovered in moss green with two big needlepoint footstools in front of it. Adam propped his feet on one of them. He'd taken off his jacket, rolled up the sleeves of his Italian silk shirt and loosened his tie to reveal the gold chain around his strongly corded neck.

Tina curled up against the pillows in the crook of the sofa's comfortable arm and waited for Adam to talk about the Generations campaign and what the venture meant to him, for that's what she expected to hear.

He did mention the campaign, but not as a successful businessman chalking up yet another coup. He talked about it from the viewpoint of a boy who'd grown up in Meadville, Pennsylvania, the son of Pavlo Kowalski. As he talked, the Kowalskis became a real family, and for the first time she began to understand something about Adam.

Under the patina of sophistication, under the hard veneer of ambition, the image of another Adam Cole began to emerge, a man more real, more vulnerable and in many ways more dangerous, for he was a man who could touch Tina's heart. She didn't want that; she was here to be his model, to represent Generations. There was no place in her plans during this brief time in New York to be emotionally moved by a man, particularly not this man, who, in spite of his newly revealed warmth, was also very, very complicated.

Tina listened quietly while Adam told her about the little boy who grew up in the shadow of the steel mills. He sipped from a glass of brandy, looking over at her occasionally and smiling, relaxed and at ease. When he turned back to the fire, she was able to study his face in profile, his smooth brow, strong chin, chiseled mouth, features that gave him a classic look—except for his nose. Its imperfection made his face more real and even more attractive. She expected it had been broken more than once and found that she was correct.

"I was about nine years old the first time I broke it. We were playing hockey in the streets on roller skates, using broomsticks and a real puck. It was a brutal game that usually ended in some kind of injury. That day I turned at the wrong time and caught a stick right in the face." Adam shook his head. "The blow knocked me out, and when I came to, I was lying in the hall outside my parents' apartment. The other kids had rung the bell but weren't about to stick around and take the blame. My dad was out of work then and we didn't have a car, so he carried me to the hospital in his arms. I don't know how many blocks away it was—the equivalent of about two miles, I imagine."

Adam was silent for a while, staring into the fire. "He was a good man," he said finally. "Of course, I broke my nose again a couple of years later in a football game. Some of us never learn."

Tina understood then the strong family ties that had formed the tough, scrappy kid. He'd grown into a man whose silk shirts and handmade suits were slightly less than conservative, a man with a little of the wild side still in him—and a lot of the tenderness left by his father.

"Dad changed his name when he became a citizen," Adam told her. "Otherwise, I'd be Adam Kowalski, and sometimes I wonder if I should go back to the old name. It seems to fit me better. Adam Cole is the image; Adam Kowalski is the man."

"Just like Bettina and Tina," came the response.

"Exactly," he agreed. "So you can understand what I mean."

"You'd be successful no matter what your name," Tina said honestly. Nothing could stop Adam, certainly not a name. She knew it and so did he.

His dark eyes studied her intently for a moment. Whatever he saw, it didn't seem to be the faded blue terry-cloth bathrobe wrapped tightly around her, knotted at the waist and reaching to her ankles. In his eyes there seemed to be the reflection of a woman dressed in sheerest gossamer through which was revealed the fullness of her breasts, the curve of her waist and the sloping line of her thigh.

Instinctively she tugged the robe closer, surprised that it was indeed the terry robe she remembered and not the fabric he seemed to be looking through. She thought she saw the beginnings of a smile on his lips, and she looked away into the fire. There was an undercurrent in the room, unspoken, unseen, but still powerful enough to make her feel somehow expectant. It seemed to manifest itself in the crackling of the fire and the ticking of the ormolu clock on the mantelpiece. These, the only sounds in the room, suddenly became deafeningly loud.

Then Adam stirred slightly, uncrossed his legs, stretched and stood up as if preparing to leave. Tina felt some of the tension drain from her body as she rose and stood beside him to thank him once again for the flowers and the apology.

If she'd spoken then, voiced her thanks, the evening might have ended. She might have walked beside him to the door and sent him into the night with gratitude. But she didn't speak. The words were prepared, yet she didn't utter them. Instead, *he* spoke, just one word, her name.

"Tina," he said, and in that word all was lost. He touched her hand and drew her toward him, slowly, so slowly that it seemed forever when in reality it was only an instant, an instant when the whole evening became nothing more than a prologue to this, their kiss.

Chapter 7

Adam kissed her softly and tenderly as if he were afraid she'd disappear. His mouth pressed sweetly against her, his lips nibbling gently while his hands roamed her back, holding her in his warm embrace.

When at last Tina's lips opened beneath his, Adam did nothing more than savor the taste of her, drinking in the sweet heady wine of their kisses. He held her close and tasted her lips, but there was no added pressure, only gentle acceptance as he received and welcomed her into his embrace.

They stood melded together, man and woman, arms entwined, bodies swaying softly as if to unheard music. There was such tenderness in their kisses, such a peaceful calm as they clung together in the night that even the crackling of the fire and the ticking of the clock seemed to have quieted, and she could hear only the dual rhythm of their breathing.

She'd tasted his lips before and felt his kisses. There'd been a jolting spark of electricity the first time their lips had met, an awakening that frightened her and made her hold back, push away, retreat. There'd been a mystery then that was focused in the mystery of the man. Now the man seemed less enigmatic to her and his kisses more welcome.

There was a peaceful assurance and a wonderful calm in these kisses. She relaxed, melted into his arms and waited, for beyond the peace of knowing was the excitement of the unknown.

Adam's lips began the foray into the unknown as his mouth drifted from hers, across her cheek toward her ear, softly, softly, dropping kisses as light as the touch of a butterfly on a flower petal and more gentle than raindrops. He was tentative, as if exploring a wondrous territory of delight. He touched her ear, her neck, her chin, the tip of her nose and each fluttering eyelid with those light inquisitive kisses.

And the tenderness of knowing passed on to the sensuality of the unknown. His mouth and hands found new, untouched parts of her to roam, and the soft exploration turned to helplessly passionate discovery that barely kept a check on fierceness. His heart lurched with need for her.

Tina felt the need; it mirrored her own. Its power was almost frightening. She thought of trying to step away from the unknown, but Adam's strong arms wouldn't yield. They bound her tightly to him. He became a gentle captor as he spoke to her of the need that surged within him. It revealed itself in more than words; it was deliriously evident in the hoarseness of his voice, which was a deep, husky whisper in her ear.

"I wanted you the minute I walked in the door tonight," he said. "I wanted to hold you and kiss you and let you feel my need. But I knew better." He smiled. "You would have refused me—thrown me out."

"I could still refuse you," she reminded Adam softly, and they both knew it was possible for them to end it all here.

Adam's hands moved again, almost dreamily, over her body. "But you won't." It was a simple statement of fact, and all she had to do was refute it. But she didn't. She tilted back her head so that her own tender smile reflected on his face.

"No," she whispered, "I won't."

She didn't tell him that since his appearance at the door she'd been waiting instinctively for him to touch her and kiss her and hold her. There were many rational reasons to bypass such a moment. Once, recently, she'd even enumerated them to Adam. They no longer applied. She couldn't stop what was happening. Rationality meant nothing beside the excitement of being in his arms. She wanted him with an aching certainty that transcended doubt and fear. She didn't tell him that, but she didn't need to. He knew.

He ran his hands through her auburn hair. Straying wisps, out of place, curled over her cheek and caught in the corner of her mouth. He brushed them back and then kissed the lips that had captured the curls. It was a kiss soft at first and then filled with sudden hunger.

Just as hungrily, Tina's tongue sought Adam's, teasing, touching, advancing and retreating until his own tongue followed and nestled in the sweet confines of her mouth.

She held him there, her hands around his neck, pressing him to her firmly, keeping him in the endless, mindless kiss from which peace had long ago fled to leave behind the bright thrust of primordial passion.

When their lips parted, Adam's hands wandered to her waist; loosened the sash of her robe and slipped inside to touch her burning flesh. She shivered violently at the touch. He felt her trembling, and it made him hesitate.

"Tina, don't be afraid," he said gently.

She held on to him, saying nothing. It had been so long, too long, since a man's hand had touched her bare skin that the touch seemed like the first one, and she felt like an innocent girl again. The memory was so old that everything was suddenly new.

"Tell me, Tina, what is it?" Urgency mixed with concern was in his voice.

She buried her head against his shoulder and trembled a little. "There's been no one since Bryant, since my husband."

He held her closer and then cradled her in his arms. "So much beauty," he said gently, "to be alone so long." His hands moved upward across her back and down again, sliding along her backbone, touching each vertebra and then cupping her firm bottom and raising her up a little to meet his own seeking body.

"Your skin is like silk," Adam whispered. "You feel so good beneath my hands, better even than I'd imagined. And I'd imagined perfection, Tina. You're more than that," he said with wonder in his voice. "More than perfection."

Tina barely heard his words of praise and affection, for she was intoxicated by his hands. His voice was merely a sound, low and sexy, that accompanied his touch, and the touch was nearly too much for her to bear.

His hands moved to her shoulders and pulled the robe away, letting it slip down her arms and fall to the floor. Naked, she stood before him, the robe a dark shadow at her feet. She glowed in the firelight that played across her long, slim legs, dappled her abdomen and highlighted the thrust of her breasts. It shone in her hair and made her eyes dark, luminous pools. Adam caught his breath when he looked into her eyes, wondering at their deep blue color. Then he looked down at the rest of her—for the first time, seeing what the firelight illuminated for him.

He took a step backward so he could see all of her, and then he reached out to touch. His wondering hands, strong and tanned against her pale flesh, explored her as if stunned by the beauty they found. Tina shivered again involuntarily and then wondered wildly how she could be cold when her flesh was on fire.

With one step he moved back to her and cupped her breasts in his hands, moving his thumbs against her nipples, working rhythmically until they hardened beneath his touch. Tina closed her eyes, letting the sensations of need and desire surge uninhibited through her as his hands moved downward to trace the line of her ribs, to measure her waist, to traverse the length of her hips and lightly skim across the joining of her thighs.

Tina opened her eyes and looked at him. Once she'd wondered what it would be like to feel his hands on the bare skin of her body, and now she knew. She knew! It was more than fantasy as Adam's strong, masculine hands discovered her secrets, exploring her and loving her. With a moan, she leaned against him and held him tightly before her hands began their loving work.

With shaking fingers Tina loosened his tie, pulled it from beneath his collar and tossed it on the floor. She fumbled with the buttons of his shirt and managed to get them undone, tugging the shirttail from his trousers and then pulling the shirt off his shoulders and arms. She let it drop, joining his tie—and her robe—at their feet.

His chest was wide and muscular; his shoulders were broad and sloping. The muscles in his arms were long, not bulky, and his abdomen was flat; she could even see the muscles there. She'd known he kept in shape, but she hadn't expected such a perfect physical specimen. Tina put her hands on his shoulders and held him as he was holding her while they continued to explore each other with wondrous eyes.

She touched the gold chain around his neck. It was cold beneath her fingers, but the skin was hot, as hot as hers. She moved her hands across the crisp, dark hair on his chest, caressing him with fingertips that searched instinctively for those areas that were the most sensitive to her loving touch. As her fingers lightly massaged his nipples, she heard his intake of breath and saw the sensuous pleasure on his face.

She would have continued her search for his places of pleasure, but he bent his head toward her in need and hunger to kiss her once again. Drawing her mouth into his and devouring her lips, he used his tongue to telegraph the need that swelled inside him.

Then suddenly he pulled back. "It's not too soon for you, is it, Tina?" His every thought was of her, for her, because he was aware that her emotions must have been locked up tight through all these years. He didn't want to break down the door that held them back; he needed to open it slowly and carefully, understanding that this could be almost like the first time.

Tina tried to answer him, but she could only shake her head. She'd never been so ready for love before.

He swept her up into his arms and holding her long, lithe frame against his chest, Adam went down the hall into the bedroom. The curtains were open and a little sliver of moonlight had trickled through the surrounding buildings, into the window and across the four-poster bed. Still holding her snugly, he pulled back the bright patterned quilt and laid her gently on the crisp sheets. They were cool, so cool that her hot body seemed to singe at the touch of her skin against them.

Adam bent over and kissed her mouth again, quickly, fleetingly, as he pulled off the rest of his clothes. He was anxious now, barely able to wait for the naked flesh of their bodies to touch at last. And when he lay beside her and Tina turned to take him in her arms, the thrill was more than either of them had expected. They gave themselves to the ecstasy of it, touching, holding, tasting, feeling—flesh against aching flesh.

Stretched out side by side on the firm bed, there wasn't an inch of her skin that didn't meet his—meet and catch fire. He wrapped her in his arms, his wide chest against her soft breasts, thighs molded to thighs, abdomen against abdomen.

Their lips met and meshed; their breaths mingled. All their senses reawakened, alive and pounding through their veins: tasting—tongues on salty-sweet skin; inhaling—nostrils filled with the musky scent of desire; speaking and hearing the words of passion's need.

The emotions that through all the years Tina had kept hidden behind a wall of reserve began to crumble under the sensory onslaught of Adam's expertise. The dam was bursting while every feeling inside her was growing, building, cresting.

She felt his hot mouth move to her breast, and suddenly she knew how she longed for that sensation. Deliberately he caressed her taut, rose-pink bud with his lips, sucking gently and then nibbling with his teeth, changing the rhythm and the tempo, letting the waves of sensuality build and then recede within her. Tina writhed beneath him. Her hands threaded frantically through his crisp dark hair as she held his head to her breast, reveling in the sensations that whirled around and around until they centered in a sweet ache at the triangle of her desire.

Emotional eons had passed since she'd felt that terrible and wonderful need that she knew—at last—would be satisfied. But not yet, not yet. There was still so much to discover, so much to experience of each other. While his lips teased her breast, Adam's hand slid down her hip, across her stomach to the edge of her feathery curling hair and then, millimeter by millimeter, downward in search of the center of her desire, the sweet budding of her need. Skillful fingers brought her to the edge of ecstasy before moving swiftly away to caress the soft skin of her inner thigh. Just as she managed to catch her breath, his fingers were there again, tantalizing, causing her to twist and turn beneath him.

How long he continued this assault on her passions, Tina couldn't tell; a moment or an eternity—she didn't know. She'd lost all track of time and space. There was only one reality; that was Adam, his mouth and his hands.

There was a sweet pause then as Adam gathered her in his arms, stopping to let them both breathe again. But in their breathing they inhaled the scent of each other and of desire, and Tina's hands reached for him, moving across his flat abdomen to the line of his hip and below. There, waiting for her, was his manhood, hard and yet silky soft beneath her questing fingers. She slipped her hands around him, murmuring words of endearment, words so long unspoken, words that unhesitatingly voiced her need.

It was a need fiercely remembered and fiercely desired. She'd waited a long time; no one—until Adam—had been able to bring that need back from memory to reality. And he brought it back now completely as he whispered in her ear, describing erotic visions of what was to come, visions that mingled with the touch and feel and scent of him.

"Tina, I can't wait any longer; I need you so," he said at last.

"Oh, Adam, I can't wait, either." She was ready for him now, eager and hungry with need.

He swung around until he was above her, and Tina opened to him like a flower to the sun. Like the petals of the roses that he'd brought to her, she opened and welcomed him.

He slid easily into her warm and welcoming softness as if he were meant to be there. At first he seemed content just to be a part of her, encased by her loving sheath. His hands held her shoulders; his eyes, darker than midnight, looked into hers as he lowered his face and kissed her—eyelids, the line of her nose, the sweep of her cheek, the fullness of her lips. He kissed her again and again until his passion could no longer be held in check and he began to move within her.

At first his thrusts were slow and easy, in perfect control to extend the moments of pleasure for both of them. But when Tina began to move with him, her hips rising to meet him, her hands gripping his back, her nails digging into his flesh, Adam's movements increased. He dove deeper and deeper into her depths. The gold chain swayed around his neck with each movement of his lithe muscular body, each thrust of his manhood.

Tina felt the pounding of the waves. Their unleashed power crested within her, struggling to break the bonds. Faster and faster they moved together, their bodies slippery with perspiration, breaths rasping, hearts racing. She opened her eyes wide and looked at Adam above her, and his black eyes penetrated her with a look such as she'd never known, a look that sparked with passion for her.

Still, the wave rose, undulating. She could no longer resist as it bore her along; she could no longer hold back the pressure building inside. She let go and rode the wave to its crest, balanced atop it for an endless moment and then let its long silken ripples wash over her. Adam rode that same passionate wave, and at the moment that she gave herself to it with uncontrollable quivering, he filled her with his essence.

Time was still unmeasurable, even now when it seemed to have slowed down. She didn't know how long they lay there, without speaking, his warm body covering hers, before he moved and gathered her in his arms. Still without words, Adam kissed her hair, her face, her throat. Tina's hand trailed lightly up the broad muscles of his back to nestle in his dark hair. It was damp to her touch. That, thought Tina, was the first sensation she could identify since that moment—hours ago or just seconds ago—when they'd ridden the wave of their desire together.

"I'm glad you didn't throw me out," he whispered.

"I'm glad, too," Tina said, hardly daring to believe that they could speak so casually after what had happened between them. Yet as casual as the words sounded, he still held her with the same feeling as before, held her quietly for a long time. Then his lips began to nuzzle her in the curve between her neck and shoulder. "Mmm, you taste good there," he teased, "but no better than in the other places. You taste good all over."

"So do you," she said almost shyly, remembering the savor of his skin on her tongue.

His hand touched the curve of her breast and then cupped it. "And fortunately, you're not skinny like most models."

"I thought you wanted me to lose weight."

"Did I say that?" he teased.

"Yes. Ten pounds, if I recall."

"Hmm. I better check this out." His hand left her breast and strayed to her waist and hip before coming to rest on her bottom. "You're sure I said ten pounds?"

She nodded again in his chest. "I've already lost six."

"Then I'll have to admit I was off a few pounds," he said, letting his hands reexamine her body from top to bottom.

"Do you mean Adam Cole was wrong?" she teased.

"Only by four pounds. Anyone can make a mistake," he added, pulling her close. "But you're certainly perfect now. Don't lose another ounce—no matter *who* dictates it." He kissed her again, a long, long kiss.

In the silence that followed, he lay back, close to her but still not touching. Tina wondered if he was going to leave her then, get up, put on his clothes and disappear with a brief kiss and a pat to acknowledge what had passed between them. She held her breath, waiting.

Finally, she was able to breathe again, aware that he was still with her—sleeping soundly. She nestled her head in the crook of his arm and soon Tina, too, was asleep. Sometime during the night they woke and made love again, no less passionately but with a deeper understanding of each other.

The insistent ringing of the telephone woke her the next morning. She tried to snuggle back into the warmth of Adam's body only to find that this time he *was* gone. She looked at the clock: 8:00 A.M. She knew that he went to the office early, much earlier than anyone else on his staff. She sat up groggily but expectantly in bed, pushed her hair away from her face with one hand and with the other reached for the receiver, hoping Adam was calling to say good-morning.

"Tina, it's Eli."

She tried to keep the disappointment out of her voice. "Eli, it's only six in the morning out there—

what's the matter?'' Disappointment began to give way to foreboding.

"Nothing really serious. I just wanted to get you before the guests came down to breakfast—and before you took off for exercise class.''

"I'm not going today,'' Tina said, having decided only at that moment to hang around a little while in the hope that Adam would call. He was still uppermost in her mind, even above problems of the inn. And there were problems; that much she knew. Eli would never waste a long-distance call on a mere chat.

"Well, serious or not, let's have it,'' Tina said, trying to concentrate on the matter at hand even though she was surrounded by memories of Adam and the night that had just passed.

There was a pause at the other end, and then a sigh and then an apology. "We hated to call; thought we could handle this one ourselves . . .''

Tina's mind ran through the previous tragedies, all of them easily worth a 6:00 A.M. phone call, wondering which one it would be. "Shall I guess?'' she asked, trying to add a little humor.

Eli laughed. "No, I'll tell you. It's the freezer. Went out with a bang. We lost a lot of meat,'' she added.

Tina sighed. That one she hadn't expected. "Good old reliable freezer that never gave us a moment's trouble. Year after year, chugging along . . .''

"Yeah,'' Eli said. "But just like the one-horse shay, when it died, it really died. The motor just gave out, and Kam couldn't repair it. We got an estimate from the repair shop.'' She named an astronomical sum.

"Good Lord,'' Tina said. "We could almost buy a new one for that.''

"Just what I had in mind." Eli was ready with another estimate.

"Okay, let's do it. I'll put a check in the mail." Silently she thanked Generations for the large advance that was already in the bank. "But save what you can of the meat," she added, having learned to think frugally. "Spaghetti sauce, stew..."

"Don't worry; Kam's already started cooking."

Tina could imagine Kam, his blue apron wrapped around his slim body, stirring the big pots on the stove. "You know," she said suddenly, "I'm homesick—for Timberline, for you and for the mountains. If we get a break in shooting, I may just get back there for a weekend."

"Hey, that's fantastic." Tina waited while Eli shouted the news down the hall toward the kitchen and Kam.

"Eli, I said *if*..."

Ignoring that, Eli came up with a suggestion. "I know!" she said with childlike enthusiasm. "Come home for your birthday."

"If it works into my schedule," Tina persisted.

"Kam'll make a stupendous birthday cake—better even than last year."

Tina remembered last year's multilayered chocolate effort. "Well, tell him not to start baking yet," she warned. "I'll let you know." But Eli was already planning. So was Tina.

Curling back into the pillows after she hung up, Tina realized how much she did miss home. It was real, devoid of backbiting and game playing; and certainly there was no fantasy about Timberline. Fully awake now with the light of the October sun streaking through the windows, Tina began to wonder whether last night had been just another example of a New York charade.

But her feelings, at least, had been real. They came soaring back when she closed her eyes, shivering even now at the memory of Adam's hand upon her breast, his hungry, greedy mouth on hers, his body holding her close. Never had she felt such need—or such satisfaction when the need was quenched.

Tina swung her feet over the edge of the bed and stood up, looking around. This room, too, had its share of flowers. Adam had placed rose filled vases on the bureau, the desk and the bedside table, where they were brightly in full bloom, further evidence—if any was needed—of what had happened. She'd made love, long, endless love to Adam Cole—the man she'd sworn to avoid. More than the fragrance of flowers reminded her; his scent was all over her skin.

Tina planted her feet on the bare polished floor and padded to the bathroom, where she flipped on the light and looked at herself in the mirror. She could see no evidence of the remembered feelings. She hadn't been magically transformed, Tina mused. Except for her tangled hair and slightly bruised lips, she was still the same thirty-five-year-old woman she'd been the day before. There was no glow surrounding her, no excitement written all over her face, no glimmer in her eyes. Nothing had changed except her sense of values, her code, her vow: she'd slept with her boss.

Silently she asked the reflection in the mirror if she'd been a fool; the reflection looked back with clear blue eyes and an obvious answer. Adam had won his power play. She'd given him exactly what he wanted— Tina, in his bed and in his campaign, not necessarily in that order. The reflection told her the hard truth: she was a fool.

Tina turned on the water and stepped into the stinging spray of the shower, angry at herself not so much for what she'd done as for the lingering feelings that were still with her. She'd turned up the phone before getting into the shower—just in case. She waited for him to call. The woman in her, loving and caring, waited.

And she wanted to believe that he cared, even though he'd left her without a word. If she was hurt, she couldn't be angry with him. Adam had made no pretenses about his appearance at her apartment: he'd wanted to woo her back to Generations, and he'd as much as said so. The flowers and the apology had been to that end. But the rest—the man who rolled up his sleeves and made himself at home in her kitchen, who talked candidly of his childhood, who seemed so gentle . . . had all of that been part of the same ploy?

She hadn't believed it then; she didn't want to believe it now. She wanted to believe that he'd made love to her because he cared about *her*, not Bettina, not his product. As the hot water rushed over her, Tina tried to wash away the nagging self-doubt that seemed determined to insinuate itself inside her brain. Why couldn't she believe in Adam? More important, why couldn't she believe in herself?

She knew why. She'd waited a long time for love, and now she was afraid that her many-splendored night had been just another night for Adam Cole. She was afraid that she'd been used.

All right, Tina told herself as she got out of the shower and dried her body vigorously with the towel, she could survive this little bit of New York game playing, if indeed that's what it turned out to be. So she'd slept with the boss. Well, it wasn't the end of the world.

Wrapping herself in the towel, she headed for the closet and picked out one of her most smashing outfits, acquired through the generosity of Century Cosmetics. What she needed was a little fun, some company for lunch to take her mind off last night and put the world in perspective. She picked up the phone. What she needed was Kay.

"This is sinful, absolutely sinful," Kay said, finishing off the last bite of chocolate mousse.

"But well deserved," Tina replied as she dipped her dessert spoon into a crystal bowl filled with macaroon soufflé. "Lord knows I work out hard enough at the club."

"And it shows," Kay commented. "You're looking very . . . healthy."

Tina dropped her eyes. Had Kay seen something that her own mirror refused to reveal? A little wary, Tina finished her soufflé before looking up again. Meanwhile, Kay had hopped right onto another train of thought, which was loosely connected to Tina's rejuvenation. "Now that you're back in the groove," she was saying, "I imagine you're ready to accept some other offers."

That was ample reason for Tina to look up at her friend, forgetting the slight blush that had dusted her face moments before. "Oh, no," she said, shaking her head forcefully.

Kay, as was her style, paid little attention. "Just listen to me for a minute. You're exclusive with Century for cosmetics, of course, but I've already begun to get other offers. Seventh Avenue is all agog. Designer lines, furriers, jewelers—they've heard Bettina's back, and they're panting for her."

For a moment Tina let that bit of news comfort her. It wasn't such a bad feeling to know that she was being sought after again, but it was nothing compared to the knowledge that when this job was over, she could go home.

"No," she repeated. "I came east to make enough money on this one campaign to fix up my inn." She looked at Kay over her coffee cup; then she took a sip of the rich brew with satisfaction and with equal satisfaction reminded Kay, "I'll have the money, and just as I promised, I'll take it and run."

Kay shrugged off Tina's refusal philosophically. "You'll change your mind."

"No, I won't," Tina said firmly.

Kay pushed aside her coffee cup, put a cigarette in her ebony holder and lit it thoughtfully. "Well, I don't plan to give up, but I am thankful for one thing—at least you're not going to walk out on Generations. It looked like touch and go there for a while, especially when I heard through the grapevine that you and Adam were shooting daggers at each other during that ridiculous filming on top of some unfinished skyscraper...."

"Don't worry, Kay," Tina responded. "I promised to behave, didn't I?" Without waiting for an answer, Tina assured her agent, "I *am* behaving."

"Oh, I know that now."

Tina looked up with a frown.

"Talked to Bill Fontana just before I left the office. I told him you and I were having lunch. I guess he thought I was privy to the *latest* argument—the one you got into with Adam after the insert shooting yesterday." Kay paused to scold Tina, "You must keep me up on these little goings-on, honey; after all I'm your agent, not to mention your friend. Anyway, he assured me that it had all worked out." Kay's lips curved in a smile that spoke volumes. "I see that he was right."

Kay would have needed to be very quick to see the light go out in Tina's eyes. But it was gone. Although Tina smiled, behind the smile her voice was tight. "Yes," she said, "it worked out just fine." She refused to let herself imagine what Adam had told Bill— or that he might have told him everything.

"Great. Then let's go shopping. On the way over, I saw a marvelous little Louis XIV table that would be perfect for my foyer. It's in a store at the corner of Madison and—"

"I don't think so," Tina declined. "I really want to get back home. They've probably seen yesterday's rushes by now, and I need to be available in case there're any problems." Tina couldn't believe what she was saying—that even after what Kay had told her, she still wanted to go home and wait for Adam's call.

"Oh, don't worry about that, honey. They won't reshoot without Adam, and he's already left."

Tina looked up. "Left?"

"For the West Coast. He'll be out there a few days. That's what Bill called to tell me."

As soon as Tina got home, she went to the window and flung it open. The scent of flowers was no longer seductive. Instead, it was cloying, the odor heavy and oppressive. And there was an air of something contrived about the rooms full of flowers, as if a theater piece had been acted out here. The flowers were part of the theatricality; although real, they seemed as artificial as Adam Cole. His little play had been perfectly planned, and she'd acted out her role as he'd written it for her, supplying the setting, complete with romantic firelight, and falling right into his arms.

Tina stood by the window, her head pressed against the cool pane, and tried to sort out what Kay had told her. Actually, it was simple enough. Adam had met with Bill at the office before leaving for his trip. He'd told Bill about the argument last night and his determination to save the Generations campaign. He'd probably explained how he'd come after her, his arms laden with flowers, his words filled with apology—the president of Century Cosmetics doing his part for his company. And of course, he would have mentioned that he'd read her quickly as a vulnerable, lonely woman who was drawn to him as every woman was drawn to him. Had he told the rest, she wondered, how he'd decided to make love to her and gain the ultimate control? It didn't matter whether he'd told or not; Bill knew, just as Kay knew.

But only Tina knew what to do about it. Disgusted, she began to remove the flowers from their vases, tearing at the delicate petals without the slightest compunction. She'd made everything easy for Adam, Tina admitted as she dumped an armload of flowers into a plastic trash bag. As soon as he'd touched her, she'd melted into his arms and given herself to him, quickly and easily.

Tina took another trash bag into the bedroom and systematically dumped the roses into it. How easy it had all been for him. A few hundred dollars' worth of flowers, some sweet words, a quick night of love before taking off for California. How easy it had been for a practiced manipulator like Adam Cole when confronted by a naive fool like Tina Lawrence.

Well, just as she was cleaning out the flowers, disposing of them with great satisfaction, so could she get rid of her memories and their accompanying schoolgirlish shivers of delight. The mirror was right; she'd been a fool. But no more.

Her first instincts about the man had been correct, and from now on she'd follow them, keeping her distance—and keeping out of his arms. Oh, she'd work for him. The phone call from Eli only reinforced the need to complete her contract. She belonged to Adam Cole until the campaign was over, but as his model, not as his woman.

Tina dumped out the last bunch of flowers and dragged all of the trash bags out the door and into the hall, where with great satisfaction she threw them, one by one, down the chute into the incinerator.

Chapter 8

I still say Paul has a crush on you." Holly whispered to Tina between lifts on the double-shoulder machine.

Next to her, struggling to reach the count of ten on the leg press, Tina could only shake her head in objection. Then falling back with aching thighs she looked over at Holly. "Don't be silly. He thinks of me as a challenge."

"That's what I said," Holly answered with a giggle.

"No, Holly, a challenge to his aerobic and nutritional theories."

"Shh. Here he comes." Quickly, Holly aligned her shoulders and smoothly lifted her elbows under Paul's dictatorial gaze.

"No talking, girls," he cautioned. "Breathe in, Holly. Hold it. Breathe out. There you go. By the way, did I mention anything about your high-density and low-density level proteins?''

Still concentrating on her breathing, Holly shook her head.

"We'll need to have a nutritional talk tomorrow," Paul decided. "Now switch machines," he barked, and they obliged quickly. "One more set each, and you're finished for the day." He began counting as Holly and Tina, sweating profusely after more than an hour under his tutelage, managed to get through their last set.

"Hold it, hold it," he demanded until they each turned purple in the face. "Okay, let down easily. That's it for today. Remember, do your cool down exercises before you get into the pool, girls," he cautioned, adding, "You're looking good, Tina," as he strode toward the lobby for his next client.

"Did you hear that? 'You're looking good, Tina,'" Holly said in a macho voice that perfectly aped Paul.

Tina shook her head as she picked up her towel and started for the locker room.

"I mean it, Tina," Holly said, following after her. "Every man you meet goes ga-ga over you: Paul, Bill, Fontana…"

"Really, Holly! Bill thinks of me as the Generations Woman, period."

"Just check out the glint in his eyes next time we're on the set, Tina." She began enumerating from her list again, "Paul…Bill…my dad, of course, although you've rebuked him—I think," she added, glancing over at Tina, who didn't respond as they pushed through the green-striped doors.

"It's nonsense." Tina sank onto the long wooden bench. "Besides, Paul's a little young. Just about right for you, Holly, dear."

Holly laughed. "Can you imagine what my father would say if I even went out with him? Lord, he'd have a stroke—'my daughter dating a...a...fitness instructor'!"

Tina pulled off her headband and shook her long hair free, dabbing at her forehead with a towel. "What type of boys does he approve of for you?"

Holly shrugged. "None that I know of, but then I don't go out so much he doesn't have anything to worry about." Holly peeled off her leotard. "I'm sort of a freak, you know. Guys are real turned off by me."

"I'd think they would be lining up."

Holly laughed. "Hardly. In fact, when there's a prom or anything like that, I never get asked. I don't know," she shrugged. "They probably think I'm dating college men or too stuck-up to go to school stuff or whatever. Come on, let's get in the Jacuzzi for a while—*without* doing our cool down," she added with a giggle.

Tina followed Holly across the green-tiled floor, and the rest of their day was spent companionably luxuriating in all the club had to offer. But Tina couldn't get over her nagging concern for the girl. Holly was lonely. Tina had felt that instinctively after only a short time, and now Holly was reconfirming it. She worked long hard hours, went to school, exercised and spent the rest of the time being watched over by her father. She didn't have a boyfriend, rarely had a date, from what she'd told Tina, and wasn't even friends with the girls at school. Holly's loneliness was further confirmed at the end of the day when she asked Tina to spend the evening with her.

"At least come and have dinner," she begged when Tina seemed hesitant. "At my apartment—my dad's apartment," she corrected.

"I don't think—"

"Dad's out of town," Holly said quickly, "so you don't have to worry." Her eyes twinkled a little. "Actually, you never did say what was going on between you two...."

"I work for your father, Holly. That's it." Tina wasn't lying; she was only stating the facts as of the day before, when she'd determined the scenario for future dealings with Adam.

"Hmm." Holly grinned and shrugged. "Whatever you say. Anyhow, he's in L.A. or somewhere on business, and it would really be fun if you'd come over." Her blue eyes pleaded.

Tina tried to think before she answered. If she was planning to keep her relationship with Adam Cole strictly business in the weeks ahead, it might be wise not to get too close to his daughter.

"I get tired of eating with the housekeeper," Holly interrupted Tina's thoughts as they left the building and stepped onto the sidewalk crowded with rush-hour pedestrians. "Mrs. Dale spies on me, you know. Reports to Dad what I do when he's gone, so sneaking out is impossible. I get real bored with her stories about crime in the streets that she gets straight from the *New York Post*. Please, Tina, I need a break tonight."

In spite of Adam, Tina liked Holly; their friendship shouldn't suffer because of her father. As Tina stood in the middle of the sidewalk trying to make up her mind how to respond, Holly suddenly disappeared.

Looking around, she discovered the girl had been all but swept away by a gaggle of teenage fans, giggling and screaming. Tina stood aside and watched as Holly handled the crowd of devotees with the aplomb of someone twice her age, answering questions about makeup and diet and signing her autograph on shopping bags, magazines and theater programs—whatever was available. Finally she broke away and headed for the street to hail a cab.

"Come on, Tina," she called, "hurry before another crowd spots me." She reached in her tote and pulled out a pair of sunglasses, which she donned quickly just as a cab pulled up. "Tina..."

"Dinner sounds great," Tina decided, opening the cab door. "Does the notorious Mrs. Dale abide by Paul's 'high-density, low-density level proteins'?"

"Only when Dad's around to keep an eagle eye on her. When it comes to food, she *can* be gotten to," Holly said with a wicked grin, "and tonight's the night."

The dinner was horribly fattening and illegal, as Holly had promised: lasagna, garlic bread, salad with a creamy mayonnaise dressing and—Holly's addition after Mrs. Dale had served the meal and disappeared back into the kitchen—a glass of Chianti for Tina, from which Holly sneaked a big sip.

"Paul would have a fit," Tina said after they'd demolished everything and returned to the living room.

"What Paul doesn't know won't hurt him." Holly sprawled on one of the long L-shaped sofas in front of the fireplace and sighed deeply. "Why is the forbidden always so much better?"

Tina smiled wryly. "Since Adam and Eve, no one's ever come up with the answer to that. If I knew the answer..." Tina wasn't quite sure what she meant. But she was afraid it had something to do with Adam, and she dismissed the thought quickly.

Holly plumped up the pillows behind her head and sighed. In her jeans and pullover sweater, she looked like any American girl settling down for a long intimate talk with her best friend. Except she wasn't any girl; she was one of the most stunningly beautiful girls in the world—and her "best friend" was twenty years older, the model who was cast as her mother.

Tina sat back in the Danish-modern armchair, perfectly at ease but with the feeling that in the silence following their exchange, Holly had become suddenly shy. Tina surmised that it was the shyness of a girl who wanted to talk, share her thoughts with a new friend, but didn't know just how to start. Tina had no idea what was on Holly's mind, but she decided to give the girl time to get her thoughts together while she carried the conversation. It could go in just about any direction. Thinking that Holly probably wanted to talk about herself, Tina began with the apartment, an easy innocuous choice but one that could evolve into Holly's life here.

"I really like this place," Tina said. And she did; it was decorated in shades of cream and blue and furnished with a mixture of modern and antique that worked beautifully. The paintings, too, were a wonderful blend that included a Dali lithograph and a Corot oil.

"Yeah, it's nice," Holly agreed. "You're surprised, aren't you," she asked slyly, "that Dad would have a place like this?"

Tina opted for honesty. "Yep, very."

Holly laughed with delight. "I'll bet you imagined black velvet and tiger skins and red satin—"

"With toreador pictures on the wall—"

"And round beds," Holly prompted.

Tina, who'd joined in Holly's game, drawled suggestively, "Well, I haven't seen his bedroom."

Holly started to giggle. "I could give you a tour." She made a move to get to her feet and was stopped only by a wave of Tina's hand.

"Maybe it wouldn't be a good idea for us to go poking around in your father's room."

Holly giggled again. "I guess not, but I can describe it. There's pecan paneling and real pretty mahogany furniture. Neat paintings, too. Sure you don't want to have a peek?" She waited for the shake of Tina's head. "Then I'll tell you a secret," she said with another smile. "He hired a decorator."

Tina nodded knowingly. "The best one money could buy."

"You've got it," Holly agreed. "But lots of the ideas were Dad's. I know, I know," she said, sure that Tina had her doubts. "The gold chain, the silk shirts and all that don't exactly go with this apartment, but I really think the other stuff is part of his image as a wheeler-dealer playboy."

"Or maybe it's a hangover from his early life," Tina suggested, thinking of the boy growing up in the shadow of the steel mills.

"Could be. When you're a poor kid like that, I guess you could have all sorts of ideas about the good life. But he's got great taste now. Course, Mom helped a lot." She paused for a moment as if wondering whether she should continue, and during that pause Tina realized that this may be what Holly had been leading to; she'd probably wanted to talk about her mother all along.

"My mom's taste is what they call 'top drawer' where she comes from," Holly said jokingly but with a tone that was clearly admiring.

Tina waited, aware that this was where the girl meant to take their conversation and wondering what would come next. She didn't have to wait or wonder very long.

"Would you like to see her picture?" Before Tina could answer, Holly was up and out of the room. She returned with a photograph of a beautiful woman with dainty, almost patrician features. There was a look of Holly in the set of her head and the molding of her eyes.

"She's lovely."

Holly nodded agreement. "This picture was taken a long time ago. I haven't seen her in—oh, almost two years, I guess. I had a shoot in Rome when I was fourteen, and she just happened to be in Italy at the time and came down to see me one afternoon." Holly gazed intently at the photograph in the silver frame as if she could somehow will it to life.

Impulsively, Tina reached for the girl's hand. "You miss her, don't you?"

"Yeah, I guess I do. I mean, not having a mom, you know. But Dad thought I'd be better off here than flitting around Europe with her. So they had this huge custody fight, and he won." Holly heaved a sigh that Tina couldn't interpret.

"And you've only seen each other once since then?"

Holly nodded.

"Do you write often?"

Holly thought about that for a minute, as if it wasn't really a yes or no question. "Neither of us is much at letter writing, and Dad—well, he's never said so, but I know he's just as glad that we're not in contact."

He would be, Tina thought.

"He says he's the one I should turn to if I need anything, and all that stuff. He says I have to trust him...that he's here and Mom isn't."

Tina didn't tell the girl that she considered what Adam was doing a subtle sort of blackmail to bind his daughter to him. Tina's words were gentle when she asked, "You don't write or talk to each other on the phone at all?"

"I could write if I wanted to," Holly said almost defensively. "Dad probably wouldn't mind that much."

Tina knew better and so did the girl. But Tina wasn't surprised by the control Adam had over his daughter. The strength of his personality was a very real force in Holly's life, just as it was—had been—in Tina's. Even without making demands, Adam Cole had a way of asserting his authority.

"I know where she lives—if she's there," Holly continued. "Mom moves around a lot."

Tina couldn't tell whether that was said in sadness or in pride. "Then you could call her very easily," Tina suggested.

"I suppose so." Holly put the picture on the end table but continued looking at it. "But then Dad would see the call when the phone bill came."

Tina shrugged and mentally gave up. The girl was afraid of her father's reactions. Tina couldn't help wondering what had happened between Holly's parents to cause Adam to be so protective about his daughter. Obviously, Pam had done something to ignite Adam's wrath. But it could have been as undramatic as asserting her own wants. Adam was vindictive to those who refused to bend to him.

"I just wish this picture could come to life," Holly said with childlike fervor, staring at the photograph. "That would be so much easier. Presto, she'd be here in the room with us. Then I wouldn't have to make any decisions about what to do."

"Well, there's really no decision that has to be made now, Holly," Tina reminded her. "When you hear from your mother again—"

"But I did hear from her. I got a letter."

Tina became attentive.

"She sent it through a friend who brought it to me. I guess she thought that Dad would keep it from me— or Mrs. Dale would. She was probably right. Mrs. Dale is very loyal to my father."

Tina nodded. She didn't need to answer now; she just needed to listen.

"Mom wants me to get in touch with her, but I don't know what to do." Holly's voice was trembly. "I don't want to hurt Dad, and I sure don't want to make him mad at me, but I miss Mom." She was quiet for a moment.

"Of course you do," Tina replied automatically. How sad, she thought, that this glowing, beautiful girl was separated from her mother now in the years when she needed her most. Part of Tina wanted to step in and take Pam's place. But she knew that was impossible. She wasn't Holly's mother; she never could be. Besides, she'd be leaving New York soon, leaving Holly behind, and then Holly would be more alone than ever.

"What should I do, Tina?" Holly's question was so heartfelt that Tina was deeply touched. She knew what Holly feared: if not Adam's wrath, then the withdrawal of his affection. Obviously she adored her father and wanted to please him. But Holly had other obligations—obligations to herself. Those included the right to get in touch with her mother and even get to know her.

The most abusive parents, deprived of custody and under the aegis of the courts, had a chance to see their children. Nothing that Pam had done could be deserving of this punishment—for her or her daughter. But even as those thoughts crossed her mind, Tina knew she couldn't give advice. It wasn't her place to do so. She could only try to help Holly understand her feelings and come to grips with them. As her friend, Tina owed the girl that much.

"What should I do?" Holly repeated.

Whatever Tina's feelings—and they were very strong at this moment—she knew Holly had to make up her own mind. "What do you want to do?" she asked her. "What does you heart tell you? Sometimes if you'll just listen . . ."

"My heart tells me to get in touch with her," Holly admitted. "But I'm afraid—and not just of hurting Dad. I'm afraid she won't like me."

"Oh, Holly, of course she'll like you. You're her daughter, and she loves you," Tina said emphatically. "Never doubt that."

Tears filled Holly's huge blue eyes. "We haven't really talked since I was a little girl. The last time—two years ago in Italy—there were people around. She brought me some presents. We went for a walk. I don't remember much about what we said. It was kind of like a party."

"You're older now," Tina reminded her.

"I know," Holly said, wiping a tear away with her shirt sleeve. "In Mom's letter she asked me to call so we could talk. I don't know if I could do that, Tina. Hearing her voice...I'd get all choked up. But I could write a letter and then maybe she'd write back, and we could get to know each other again through the mail. That's possible, isn't it?"

Tina nodded.

"Dad wouldn't even have to know. She could keep sending letters through her friend."

"That's sort of sneaky, Holly," Tina advised. "Maybe if you decide to write, you should do it openly."

"I don't know if I have the nerve."

Tina understood that perfectly well. Adam Cole was a hard man to stand up to.

Tina thought about Holly all the next day. No matter what decision the girl made, whether she contacted her mother or not, problems were sure to surface. If Holly got in touch with Pam, Adam certainly wouldn't be pleased; if she didn't, Holly would always bear anger and resentment against her father.

On the way to class at the university that night, Tina still couldn't wrest her mind from Holly. She'd resisted the temptation to call the girl, knowing that would just make her appear curious. Holly's choice was clear: to tear up her mother's letter or get in touch with her. Tina was more than curious about her decision; she was genuinely concerned, and she took her concern right into the classroom.

"Mrs. Harris..." Stuart Forrester's voice finally got her attention. "Mrs. Harris, I was asking for a progress report on your Brontë paper."

Tina sifted through her notebook guiltily. "Yes, of course. I was just arranging my notes..."

"You don't have to read them to me, Mrs. Harris. Just a quick rundown of their contents."

"Yes, of course," Tina repeated, and managed to supply him with the information he wanted. But she felt obligated to stay after class and apologize.

"I could tell you were a million miles away," Stuart Forrester said with a smile in his blue eyes. "I've learned to know when I've lost a student's interest. A sort of vague look comes into the eyes—usually when I'm not in my best form. Tonight, however, I thought the class was fairly lively."

"Oh, it was," Tina agreed quickly. "It's my fault for bringing concerns about a friend to class. My mind has never wandered before, especially not during your lectures. Why, I think your class is—extraordinary."

At that, Stuart threw back his head and laughed. "I don't believe anyone has ever used quite that word before. I'm flattered." He closed his briefcase and walked beside Tina to the door. As he flicked out the light, he turned to her. "Would you like to join me for a drink or coffee? This is my heavy-schedule day—

three classes in the morning and one at night, with afternoon conference hours, so on Thursday I like to unwind a little.''

Before Tina could recover from her surprise at the invitation, Stuart had taken her arm and was guiding her down the hall. ''We'll head toward the West Village and away from the usual NYU haunts. I wouldn't want my other students to think I had a favorite. Although if I did have one,'' he admitted disarmingly, ''it would certainly be you.''

Again, Tina could only smile in surprise. While she had become a little more responsive in class, she was hardly a remarkable student.

''But for tonight,'' he continued, ''let's suspend the professor-student roles. What do you say, Tina?''

''It's a deal, Stuart,'' Tina agreed as they stepped into the crisp night.

They walked along Eighth Street, stopping to look in the coffeehouses and neighborhood bars along the way until they found a place that seemed perfect for their late-night conversation. The lights were low, and the songs from the piano were familiar but unobtrusive. It was nothing like the sophisticated club where Adam had taken her, and for that Tina was glad.

They began the evening at arm's length conversationally, even though their bodies were necessarily very close because of the cramped quarters and the minuscule table. They talked about the music, the weather, the weekend, but by the time their drinks arrived they'd gotten back to the poetry class.

Tina had heard from other students that it was the most popular evening class at the university. ''I was lucky to get in,'' she told Stuart. ''I almost didn't, you know. At the last minute, there was a cancellation, and my advisor slipped me into the spot before anyone else found out about it.''

"The dropout probably discovered the real scoop on my class," Stuart answered with a deprecating smile as their waiter, having delivered two glasses of white wine, managed to leave without getting wedged between the wall and the table.

"For whatever brought you to my class," Stuart said, "the luck is mine." He touched his glass to Tina's, and she found herself blushing. "I hope I've lived up to my reputation."

"Oh, you certainly have," Tina said as the blush faded. "I've learned so much during the past few weeks that I may not be able to retain it all. Remember, I haven't been a student for a long time. The mental faculties are very rusty."

"I wouldn't worry about that for a moment," Stuart said with an admiring smile. "You have some good ideas." After a pause, he suggested, "Why don't you come to the seminar next Wednesday and digest a little more information? Some of us will be presenting papers that might be helpful. There'll be a reception afterward," he added.

"Do you think my brain can take any more?"

"Definitely," Stuart answered. "Will you come?" His voice was eager, and Tina wondered if she'd been singled out from the others since he hadn't mentioned the seminar to the class.

"Of course. I'd love to—if it's in the evening," she added. "I may be working during the day—"

"It's at eight o'clock," he corroborated before pausing to look at her curiously. "You know, I don't have any idea what you do, where you work. I only

know you as a student—and a very interesting one—
but what about the other Tina Harris?''

She took a long sip of wine. Now she would have to
reveal Bettina, unless... She thought for a moment
about fabricating a background separate from the
modeling business, Generations and Adam Cole. But
she couldn't do that. She wanted to be honest with
Stuart, so Tina took a deep breath and told the truth.

"I'm a model. Or at least I used to be, years ago.
Now I'm making—well, I guess you'd call it a
comeback.''

In the shadowy light, Tina could see Stuart looking
at her, assessing her casual clothes—a silk blouse and
tweed skirt—and her face, which was without makeup
except for a trace of lip gloss.

"I should have guessed that," Stuart said. "You're
a natural beauty.''

Again, Tina felt herself blush as she smiled mod-
estly. Coming from her professor, the compliment
seemed very sincere.

"But I can't imagine you'd ever have to make a
comeback. You have the kind of beauty that no one
could forget.''

"Well," Tina said with a smile, "they *did* forget—
for about eight years, while my husband and I were in
Colorado.''

"And after he died, you decided to try again..." He
was fitting the pieces together.

"Necessity dictated it, let's say. Anyhow, here I am,
working again and trying to revive the old image. Except that things have changed a little. Now I'm playing the mother of a teenage girl in a campaign for
Century Cosmetics.''

"The mother? I don't believe it.''

She nodded. "It's true. Holly Cole's mother."

"Oh, yes," Stuart remembered. "I saw a segment about that young model on a morning-news program. She's very heady company—what they call a superstar, isn't she?"

"That's Holly," she agreed, relieved that—for Stuart Forrester, at least—Tina wasn't in the specious group called superstars.

"But I suppose modeling is more than just being beautiful," he added. "It must be very trying to spend such long hours under hot lights."

"Yes, it is," Tina agreed. "There's very little glamor in the actual work." She hoped the conversation wasn't going to turn into a dissection of the modeling business. She'd tried to leave that behind her and not bring it into her life as Tina Harris, and she didn't want Stuart to turn out like so many others—a celebrity watcher and collector of anecdotes about the rich and famous.

He didn't disappoint her. "I also suspect you don't like to talk about it," he said correctly, "and my class is your escape."

Tina nodded. "But it's more than that, Stuart. This world down here at NYU is like another life. It's a life that I neglected once before, and I'm not about to make the same mistake again." She looked at him under lowered eyes. "Now that you've found me out and know all about my checkered career, I do hope I'm still invited to the seminar."

Stuart laughed. "You're even more welcome than before. It's not often we ordinary college professors have celebrities in the audience."

Tina had been teasing, and so had Stuart; yet his response made her wince in the darkness. Just because of her association with Holly, Stuart had—even if jokingly—promoted her to celebrity, and something was already beginning to change. The anonimity she'd so desperately needed when she decided to attend evening classes was disappearing. At least Stuart didn't know who she *really* was; she intended to keep it that way, even though she imagined he was too young to have heard of Bettina.

Tina could hear the phone ringing as she put the key into the lock. She got it on the tenth ring.

"Tina? I was about to give up."

She should have known that only Adam would be so persistent.

"I've been trying to reach you since I left." His voice was more seductive over the phone than if he'd been here beside her, Tina realized. She felt her fortitude weaken. "I was afraid you'd gone out of town," he continued. The voice caressed her.

"No." The monosyllable was clear and firm. At least she could get one word in without letting him hear her feelings. She was determined to say whatever else was required with the same lack of emotion.

"I tried to reach you several times. Just found out that you were with Holly last night." Obviously Adam was checking up on her. She wasn't surprised. "I called earlier this evening. Around seven..." He paused, waiting for Tina to explain.

"I was out," she said. The university, her classes, Stuart Forrester were her personal and private domain, and she wasn't about to let Adam start controlling that part of her life.

There was a pause; she knew he'd heard the coolness in her voice and imagined that he was trying to figure it out. Finally, he went on as if he hadn't been rebuffed. "I'm in L.A. Had a meeting here Tuesday and another one yesterday."

"Yes, Kay told me you'd gone to the coast." Tina made a mistake then; her tone, if not her words, intimated that he should have told her about the trip himself.

Adam caught on. He tried to explain even though she hadn't asked for any explanation. "I actually forgot about the meeting until Tuesday morning. That's very unlike me," he added, "to forget a planned trip, but I was thinking about something the night before." His voice still held the sexy warmth that made her so nervous. "Tina—"

"I've taken the time while you were away to keep in shape," she inserted, cutting off what he'd meant to say next. "Holly and I spent all day yesterday at the gym," she said.

"And tonight?" he asked, still persisting.

"I was out," Tina repeated.

"Mysterious, eh?" he teased. "Makes me wonder if there's another man in your life. You know, I'd be jealous, Tina. I don't like to share my women." It was a teasing remark in the image of Adam Cole.

But if he'd expected her to take it lightly, he didn't know Tina. Bravado or not, she wasn't amused. "I'm not your woman, Adam, even in the most casual sense."

"I'd like you to be," he said with an entirely different tone. "In fact, I've been thinking about you ever since I left New York, thinking about our night together.... I wouldn't mind another one like that."

Another night, thought Tina, or two or three until the campaign was over and she went back to Colorado. In that time he would be able to touch her deepest feelings, but for Adam, she would still be just another of his women.

"I don't think so, Adam."

"Tina, why? I don't understand."

"It would be wrong to continue this. You're my boss, and becoming lovers destroys the professional relationship—"

"Come on, Tina. We've discussed that before, and we can handle it."

"Maybe you can. I can't. I won't be here much longer; the campaign is almost over. Until then, we need to pick up where we were at first, before...before..."

"What's the real reason, Tina?" His voice was demanding. "If you're leaving New York as you say, then you've got nothing to lose. You can just walk away. What the hell is it? Is it because what happened to us wasn't good for you?" His tone dared her to lie.

And unable to lie, she avoided the question. "It's because I felt used, Adam. You were afraid I might walk out on the Generations campaign, and you used me, used my needs to keep me here. I'm not sure whether it was love we were making that night or the consummation of a business deal."

There was more that Tina didn't say. If he'd cared, he would have told her and not left without a word. He left her because he'd gotten what he wanted—Tina and Generations. And a couple of days later he thought about her again and decided to call. Why not? She was available for a while, and then she'd be gone. It was a perfect arrangement for Adam Cole. Tina's feelings couldn't be treated quite so lightly.

But he heard only what she said, and the words surprised him. "If you believe that, you can't think much of me, Tina."

She didn't take it back, and after a long pause Adam apparently decided to go along with her. "Maybe you're right," he said. "Maybe our relationship should be professional." Then his voice bit with sarcasm. "Trust obviously isn't a part of this." Without another word, he hung up.

But long after he put down the phone, Adam sat on the bed in his hotel room, thinking. When he'd left her that morning, he'd bent over and kissed her lips as she slept and thought of waking her. But for the first time in his life, Adam had felt unsure. He'd given himself too completely to Tina, and he was hesitant, possibly even afraid of his feelings. So he'd left her there, gone home to change and taken his daily morning run. He could usually sort out his thoughts when he ran. But everything had still been unsettled in his head until he got to L.A. And he'd been trying to reach her ever since.

Chapter 9

Tina and Holly came off the beach shivering, and one of the crew members rushed over to cover them with blankets. Tina, wearing a halter sundress, and Holly, in cuffed shorts and a camp shirt, were filming a commercial for the new line of makeup colors for summer. Although the sun was bright and in the distance the ocean was a calm dark blue, the temperature hovered at thirty-three degrees.

Clasping the blankets around their shoulders, they ran for the trailer at the edge of the beach.

"I did it, Tina. I did what you suggested," Holly said as they entered the warm trailer and closed the door behind them.

Tina plopped down in front of an electric heater and looked at the girl with a frown.

"Oh, you know," Holly went on. "What you said. I called Mom."

Tina's mind registered only part of the sentence. "What *I* said?"

"Sure, you told me to follow my heart, and that's what I did. I went to my agent's apartment and called Mom. She was home. That was a good omen, I thought, like she was expecting my call. We talked for a long time. It was great—real easy and not at all what I expected. I think it's going to be all right, Tina—" Suddenly Holly glanced out the window and then with a quick wave headed down the hall toward the back of the trailer, chiming, "I'll go into makeup first since I'm more windblown than you."

"You told your father about the call, didn't you?" Tina shouted after her, but she had already disappeared.

The door of the trailer opened, letting in a blast of cold air—followed by Adam Cole—and Tina realized why Holly had hurried away.

The involuntary shiver that ran through Tina had nothing to do with the outside temperature. She watched Adam close the door and lean back against it. He was wearing a dark blue coat with a velvet collar, and while it wasn't appropriate for a location shoot at the beach, Tina couldn't help thinking that he'd never looked more handsome. They hadn't seen each other since the morning he left her apartment without a word, their only contact an abruptly ended phone conversation. Tina had been relieved when he hadn't appeared at the beach that morning, but only now did she realize how much she'd dreaded facing him.

"Adam." She spoke his name and tried to smile, hoping the beating of her heart wasn't audible.

"Tina," he answered in a voice as even as hers. "I'd like to drive you back to the city when the shooting wraps tonight." When she didn't respond immediately he added, "The campaign's not over yet, and we need to get a few things straightened out as we go into the last weeks. We can stop on the way for dinner," he said in a voice that seemed to demand less than it urged, although the difference was subtle.

Tina wanted to answer without any excuses, making it final between them. Instead she explained that she had an appointment, but without mentioning that tonight was Stuart Forrester's seminar.

"Then forget dinner, I'll drop you off."

"I have to change first."

"Then I'll take you to the apartment. Tina, we need some time to talk—just the time it takes us to get into the city; that's all. If there's tension between us, everyone feels it, and at this point, so late in the campaign, we can't let that happen."

Tina nodded in defeat. She couldn't deny that the undercurrents between them would affect the atmosphere on the set; she couldn't deny that these last weeks were important for them all.

"I'll be at your car after we wrap," she said obediently, and only then did Adam move away from his position at the door, heading down the hall toward the room that was set aside for the makeup department, to check on his daughter.

Adam had driven out to Long Island in his own car, and as Tina settled beside him in the little sports coupe, she was relieved that he would have to pay more attention to the road than to her. The one evening when they'd been chauffered in his limousine had been an uneasy, provocative one, and at this stage of their relationship she wouldn't want to experience anything like that again.

As soon as Adam got onto the expressway, he looked over at Tina. "I didn't like anything you had to say when I called from California," he began without preamble.

"All of it had to be said," she replied. "I'm sorry that it wasn't pleasant, but I was being honest about how I felt. I don't think that either of us will gain by playing games."

"Unless we play by your rules..." His voice had a sharp edge to it.

Determined to avoid an argument, Tina decided not to answer.

Adam returned his gaze to the road. "Obviously whatever went on between us didn't make you feel very confident about me." The setting sun was still bright, and he put on the sunglasses that had been buried in his dark hair, on top of his head. Tina looked away, reluctant to admit that watching him still made her weak. "Am I so hard to trust?" he asked.

She gave the only possible answer. "For me, yes. I can't forget that you appeared at my door at a very opportune moment—when you knew I could walk out on Generations and leave you in big trouble."

Adam shook his head. "You don't mince words, do you?"

"This is the time for honesty, Adam. Maybe if we'd tried it sooner—"

"You mean if *I'd* been honest."

Tina shrugged. "That might have saved me some hurt later on. When you didn't call that morning, when you told Bill about us—"

Adam turned back toward her then; she could see his dark eyes flashing behind the tinted glasses. "Bill knows nothing about you and me. What the hell gave you that idea?"

Tina, momentarily confused by his denial, wondered if she could have misunderstood what Kay had told her. Maybe Adam hadn't bragged to Bill . . .

Adam confirmed these doubts. "I told Bill I'd acted like a fool after the shooting and that I'd apologized to you later. That's all. Actually, Bill was floored by both confessions." Adam grinned in remembrance. "First that I'd admit a mistake and then that I'd apologize—to anyone. Maybe you're making a new man of me, Tina." Without looking at her, he reached out and took her hand.

She drew it away quickly. "Adam, please."

"Okay, okay," he said, returning his hand to the steering wheel. "But what I've told you is the truth." Digesting his words, wanting to believe, Tina hesitated a beat too long, and Adam reacted first. "I'm not used to being taken for a liar."

"I'm sorry," she said quickly. "I must have misinterpreted a secondhand version of what happened." When he looked at her again, eyes narrowed, Tina added. "I believe you, Adam."

He read beyond her words. "But you still think I was using you?"

"What else can I think?" she asked honestly. "You came to me after we'd had a very heated discussion and you—we—"

"Made love," he said for her.

"Yes," Tina whispered. "And then you left me without a word and didn't call. What else could I think?" Tina repeated the words without even hearing the plea in her own voice—a plea for the truth that would make her believe.

Adam was quiet as they reached the city and headed across town toward her apartment. Tina thought he might just drop her off at the door and that would be the end. She sat still, holding her breath, not knowing what he was going to do and not even knowing what she wanted him to do.

When Adam finally spoke, his words were carefully chosen and from the heart. "You can believe this much, Tina. I wanted you the minute I saw you. Remember that first day at David's studio? I touched your hair..."

She did remember, so well.

"I wanted to touch your face; I wanted to kiss you." Adam pulled down the sun visor, took off his glasses and looked over at her again. His brown eyes were serious. "That night after we went to the theater, you knew how I felt, and you walked away from me." The trace of a smile crossed his lips, and Adam shook his head. "Women usually don't do that. Of course, nothing about you is a surprise."

"If what you wanted had happened that night, then *you* would have walked away."

"You may be right," he admitted truthfully. "All I know is that I thought about you, desired you, but you were always just beyond my reach. When I couldn't own you, I tried to control you." He paused for a moment and then said, "I'm being more truthful now than I've ever been with anyone, Tina. I thought that making love to you that night could end my need for you. Maybe I even hoped it would. Maybe that's why I left without waking you and didn't call. I really don't know, Tina. I've never felt like that. When I couldn't think about anything but you, I finally called. I knew it wasn't over.''

"It is now, Adam. Now, before we get any more involved." Tina didn't bother with the rational reasons that they'd been over again and again; they both knew none of them really mattered. At issue was the difference between desire and love, between a man and a woman with different standards, different futures and very different goals.

Adam had parked the car in front of her apartment building and waved the doorman away. He turned off the engine, pulled up the armrest between them and turned to look at her, long and hard, now that he didn't have to concentrate on driving. He was waiting for her to finish what she'd begun.

Tina wasn't sure she could say the rest. "I cared for you, Adam," she began hesitantly, "but I needed to protect myself..."

"From what?" he pressured.

"From falling in love." She spoke boldly, her eyes holding his. "I don't need to fall in love with you, Adam, because if I did, I would get hurt. You know that as well as I."

The look in her eyes was so intense, so strong that it made him wince and look away. What she was saying was the truth as she saw it, and she didn't expect a denial.

"We're very different," Tina went on, "and we don't want the same things from life." She was talking openly of feelings she'd long ago put away, much as she'd hidden her scrapbooks high on the shelf at Timberline.

"I knew it would be that way with you," he admitted. "Love. Love or nothing?" It wasn't quite a question, but more a statement of what he thought Tina was all about.

"I'm old-fashioned, I guess," she said with a shaky half laugh.

He reached for her hand and held it. His grip was warm and strong. Tina didn't pull away. She needed the strength his touch gave her, now that she'd spoken so openly about her feelings.

"I'm not ready to make a commitment, Tina," he said, still clasping her hand. "But you know that. Isn't it what this whole conversation's about?"

She nodded. "Yes."

"Then what's left for us? We can't return to a strictly business association, not after what's happened between us. I want more than that."

"I do, too." They sat silently, holding each other's hand, and Tina ventured in a weak voice that even to her ears sounded faraway, "Could we try friendship?"

Adam laughed. "That usually doesn't work for me—friendship with women."

"You've never tried it with me," she reminded him, tilting her chin in the challenging way that had become familiar to him.

"No," he admitted, "I haven't."

"That might solve a lot of problems, Adam. We'd be more comfortable working together—and the atmosphere on the set would be more relaxed if we were able to talk honestly with each other."

"The way we've talked today..." he suggested.

Tina nodded.

Adam pretended to ponder her offer. "Suppose we became—friends," he said playfully. "I'd have to establish a few rules..."

"In the spirit of the former quarterback," Tina said with a smile, relieved that the tension between them seemed to be resolved—at least for now.

"Exactly. You'll still have to have dinner with me occasionally..."

Tina nodded.

"Maybe go the the theater..."

"Fine," she said, "but no dancing."

Adam sighed deeply. "No dancing. But there's one more thing, Tina. You'll have to trust me." He wasn't joking now.

"I deserve that, Adam, and after today—after our talk—I know that I can trust you." Tina surprised herself by what she said next. Whether because of the friendliness of their talk or her need for companionship, she found herself telling Adam about the seminar that night.

"I've been going to class at NYU in the evenings. That's why you couldn't reach me."

Adam sat back, shaking his head as if to say that just when he thought he knew her, Tina showed him yet another side.

"At school no one knows who I am. To them, I'm just Tina Harris. I told my professor—Dr. Forrester—that I was a model, but he didn't make the connection between me and Bettina. In fact, I doubt if he's ever heard of Bettina. He likes me and respects me for who I am—a student in his class and a damn good one. You can't imagine how that pleases me, Adam. I need the anonymity when I'm at school I need something for myself. Can you understand that?"

"Sure," he answered monosyllabically. He'd seen the animation in her face and realized that the class—and maybe even the professor—meant something special to Tina. Adam felt a quick stab of jealousy, cursing himself that he still wanted her but vowing to be careful not to step over the lines she'd drawn. He wasn't going to make another mistake and lose her completely. As long as they had an arrangement, however tenuous and platonic, he was determined to be satisfied.

"Could you take a guest along tonight?" he asked suddenly.

"You want to go?" She was genuinely amazed.

Adam pretended hurt. "Tina, I may not be a genius like this Dr. Foster—"

"Forrester," Tina corrected, knowing that he'd made the mistake on purpose. Adam wasn't one to forget a name.

"Just so you don't call him by his first name," Adam said. He waited for Tina to blush. She did, but he pretended he hadn't noticed. "And, yes," he added, "I'd like to go. I'm interested in more than sports and cosmetics, Tina." He raised one eyebrow. "Or would you be embarrassed to show up with an ex-jock?"

Tina smiled. "If you don't mind waiting, I'll run in and change out of these summer clothes."

The small auditorium was hot and crowded, and Tina suggested they sit at the back, thinking that Adam might not last very long.

She was wrong. He took off his topcoat and loosened his tie, but he didn't talk, complain or even shift his position on the uncomfortable chair during the long seminar. Instead, he sat quietly, listening as each paper was read and the questions were posed. He seemed to pay special attention to Stuart Forrester, watching the younger man's face, even when Stuart wasn't at the podium. Adam was like a predator stalking his prey, Tina thought with fascination and a little wariness. She couldn't help wondering if he had something planned.

Whey they left the auditorium and crossed the street to the faculty club, she decided to get a reading of what was going on in Adam's mind.

"Did you enjoy the seminar?" she asked.

"Very much," he admitted. "Particularly the paper on Byron, who happens to be one of my favorite poets—and don't say you're not surprised at my choice." He slid one arm around Tina's waist, the first time he'd touched her since holding her hand in the car.

"That paper *was* good," she agreed before getting quickly to her point. "So was Dr. Forrester's."

"Oh, yes, Forrester."

Tina glanced covertly at Adam but didn't push any further. She wasn't about to fish when he seemed determined to be so evasive.

The whole crowd had streamed across to the reception, an erudite, tweedy group made up of professors and graduate students, along with some friends and family and a few of what Tina had come to think of as intellectual groupies. The groupies were already gathered around their favorite professors, including the young and charming Dr. Forrester.

He saw Tina through the crowd and waved her over. If Stuart was surprised to see her with an escort, he hid the sentiment well.

"I'm so glad you could come, Mrs. Harris—Tina," he said as the groupies backed off a little, leaving the professor with half a dozen colleagues, Tina and

Adam—the latter two clearly intruders to the young people's way of thinking.

"I enjoyed the seminar very much," Tina told him. "You were right in saying it would be helpful. I took a lot of notes."

"I noticed that," Stuart said, and Tina felt as if she could see the knowing smile on Adam's face, but she didn't turn to look as she introduced him to Stuart.

Stuart recognized Adam immediately, causing Tina to realize that Adam Cole was a household word, even deep in academia.

"We're delighted to have you here, Mr. Cole," he said with obvious pride as he turned toward his colleagues. "I'm sure you didn't expect to have not one but two celebrities at our seminar."

Tina felt her heart sink. She'd come to NYU to study, attend class and learn without any attendant notoriety; she'd come to the seminar at Stuart's suggestion to gather information that might be helpful in putting together her paper. She saw her anonymity fading away, and to Tina's surprise, she saw Stuart as the catalyst.

He was busy explaining to a woman who'd been on the panel with him, "Tina is one of my students, Tina Harris is her name, but that's not the name you would know her by. She's actually Bettina," he said with a certain amount of personal satisfaction, as if he'd had a hand in her fame.

Nonplussed, Tina tried hard to avoid Adam's eyes, since she could imagine the twinkle there as he watched her highly touted professor turn into a fan.

"I just learned recently that Tina was a model," Stuart continued for his friend's edification. "Not until a few days later did it come to me that she was

Bettina. Remember the ad with the pearls?" he asked to the group in general as Tina's heart sank further. "As if anyone could forget that face."

His colleagues got right into the spirit, and Tina responded graciously, as her role dictated. But she felt her face flush, not with embarrassment but with disappointment. Dr. Forrester, whom she'd described to Adam as a brilliant scholar, unimpressed with the outside world, was showing her off as his personal celebrity to a group of academics whom Tina wouldn't have expected to fawn. But they were doing just that. And so was Dr. Forrester.

"There are some more people I'd like you to meet," he said. "I told them you'd be here—" he took Tina's arm to lead her away "—so I'm doubly glad you decided to come."

Tina cast a hopeful glance in Adam's direction, but he wasn't about to help out. "I'll grab us a drink," he said. "I think I see a familiar face over by the bar."

Tina cursed him silently for deserting her, but she could only blame herself. She'd offered Adam this evening so he could see the other side of her life, in the anonymity of the intellectual community. Her plan had backfired, and she couldn't blame Adam for gloating. With a resigned sigh, she followed Stuart.

An hour later Tina extricated herself from a clutch of academics who were far more interested in discussing Bettina, Holly Cole and Generations than nineteenth-century English poetry. Adam was still at the bar, deep in conversation. For a moment, before joining him, Tina stopped to look at Adam in this unfamiliar setting. The cut of his suit, the expensive leather shoes, silk shirt and gold jewelry and the year-round tan set him apart from the corduroy jackets and pipe smoking of the other men. Yet he wasn't uncomfortable or out of place. He was Adam Cole, and wherever he went, he took that persona with him.

Tina's drink was still on the bar, the ice melted. She grabbed it and took a long sip. Weak or not, she needed it. With a knowing smile Adam reached out and took her arm, put the drink back on the bar and ordered another one. Then he introduced her to the man beside him.

"This is Jim Callahan, an old friend from my college days. Believe it or not, I played football with the professor."

Tina accepted the warm handshake. "Adam and I haven't seen each other in years," Jim told her.

"Well, if you'd ever come down from your ivory tower," Adam prodded, "and stop churning out all those scholarly tomes . . ."

"Publication's the name of the game," Jim Callahan said with a shrug. "Of course, if I'd gone into pro ball . . ."

"You were lucky we let you on the college team," Adam reminded him. The two men bantered on for a while, recalling old times until Jim called a halt to the reminiscences.

"We're boring Tina with all this nonsense. Let's hear about her. What brings you to NYU and tonight's seminar?"

Before Tina could answer, Adam spoke up. "Tina's a student here, and a very serious one."

She looked at Adam and smiled.

They left the overheated club and walked through Washington Square toward the garage where Adam had parked his car. There was a bitter nip in the air, and Tina had belted her suede coat and pulled up the collar around her neck. Adam, relieved to be out of the stuffiness of the club, had draped his coat over his shoulders. Only Adam could get away with that and not seem pretentious, Tina thought as once again she forced herself to look away from him.

"So, Professor Forrester doesn't care anything about Bettina," he mused.

Tina had expected that. "Don't rub it in," she responded.

"I guess it just goes to show that all the world loves a star."

"Hmm." Tina didn't really want to talk about her disappointment in Stuart. It was enough that she felt it. "I wish I'd never told him who I was. I wish—"

"That you weren't Bettina?"

"Some of the time." They walked on, their footsteps echoing across the nearly deserted park. "Most of the time," Tina decided. "I think it really hit me— my confusion about who I am—when I saw you standing at the bar talking to Jim. You obviously weren't a part of that academic scene, and yet you fit into it perfectly without making the slightest effort. You've managed to blend your images together into one very comfortable persona."

"Not completely," Adam answered. "There're still two Adam Coles: the Kowalski kid from the wrong side of the tracks and the high-powered executive. But you're right; I'm comfortable with both of them. I like them both."

They stopped and sat down on a bench near the arch. "Does that mean you don't think I like Bettina?"

Adam put his arm around her. "I don't know whether you like her or not. She's a beautiful woman, though, with an easy star quality. But I like Tina better. The real Tina, I mean—whenever I get a chance to get close to her and know what she's all about."

The park was quiet in the chill dark night, and Adam pulled Tina closer. She looked up at his face, softly illuminated by the streetlights, as it moved closer and closer to hers. His lips almost grazed her protesting mouth.

"Adam..." She tried to turn away.

"Just a friendly kiss," he answered as his lips met hers, warm and sweet. From that moment she stopped fighting the feeling she'd been fighting most of the day...driving back from Long Island beside him, watching him across the room at the faculty club, walking with him across the square...and now, lost in his kiss.

His lips tasted like the memory she'd been carrying of him, and his tongue was warm and sweet against hers. She could think of nothing but lying in his arms, naked, with his lean hard body next to hers. Tina pushed the memory away as she put her hands against his chest and pushed Adam away, or tried to. His arms held fast, and although he released her mouth from his intoxicating kiss, his face was still next to hers, his lips close to her ear.

"I was jealous of your professor when you told me about him," he whispered. Tina drew back a little and looked up at him. His eyes were darks coals in the night, but he was smiling. "Dr. Forrester, the scholarly professor. He sounded quite formidable. During the seminar, I watched him."

"Yes, I know," Tina said with a smile.

"I was still jealous, mind you, Tina. His paper was very impressive." Tina leaned her head on Adam's shoulder and waited for him to say the rest.

"But he's only a fan, as it turns out. And he's obviously a fool, since he's chosen to be awed by Bettina—even after he's known Tina. You don't need that kind of boy. You need a man, Tina. You need me." He kissed her again, cupping her face in his two strong hands and drinking from her lips, hungrily, as if she were filled with the sweetness of nectar.

When the kiss ended, he took her hand and pulled her up from the bench. They continued walking slowly across the park, arms around each other while Tina tried to sort out her feelings. It was impossible; she couldn't think now. She needed more space. She needed to be away from him and away from New York.

"I want some time to think, Adam," she said. "We have a break coming up next week. I'd like to take a trip back home, to Colorado."

There was a long silence broken only by the accelerated beating of their hearts and the dull echo of their footsteps on the pavement.

"Don't you trust me to come back?" Tina asked, remembering their conversation about learning to trust each other.

Adam stopped under the streetlight and looked at her. "I trust you, Tina. I'm sure you'll come back to finish the campaign. That's not what I'm thinking about." He held her hand as he led her across the street to the parking structure.

A young attendant put down his magazine and took Adam's ticket stub. "It's a white BMW coupe," Adam said as the boy disappeared into the building.

Adam was still holding her hand. "What's it like back there—in Colorado?"

"It's beautiful. The air's clean. The snow's powdery. The streams are clear...."

"I'd like to go back with you. I'd like to see where you live, what you'll be returning to." When Tina opened her mouth to protest, Adam put his fingers on her lips. "If you walk out of my life—*when* you go— I'd like to have shared something special with you."

Looking up at him, Tina realized he was serious. What he wanted had nothing to do with Generations, with commitments or contracts. He wanted them to be together away from the pressures. He wanted to be with *her*.

"It's terribly cold..."

"But clean."

"The snow's—"

"Powdery. And the streams are clear."

"I don't know, Adam," she hesitated. "Timberline's not the kind of place you're used to. The accommodations..."

"Are rustic," he guessed. "You'd be surprised, Tina, how well I'll fit in. I'm adaptable, remember? But if it doesn't work out, you can send me packing."

The attendant drove up and hopped out of the car. Adam handed him a tip and opened the door for Tina. "What do you say?"

"Well..." She could feel herself wavering.

"Great," Adam said. He closed her door, went around the car, got in and released the brake. Then he looked over at her. "When do we leave?"

"You're taking Adam Cole to Colorado with you?" Kay put down the proofs she'd been perusing and fixed unbelieving eyes on Tina. Once more Kay had lured Tina to her office in hopes of persuading her to stay on in New York. Once more Tina had refused, and the two friends had moved on to talk of more personal matters.

"I'm not exactly taking him," Tina hedged. "He's going with me."

"However you phrase it, this calls for a celebration." Kay touched a panel behind her desk and a complete bar swung into view. She smiled at Tina. After all her years in the office, its expensive touches still delighted her. She dropped ice cubes into two goblets and filled them with sparkling mineral water. After handing Tina her glass, Kay looked at her speculatively. "So my instincts were right. There is something going on between you and Adam."

Tina felt herself flush and wished she had the power to control that unfortunate reaction. "*Was*, Kay. We had a...a..."

"Fling?" Kay supplied.

Tina smiled. "That's a polite word for what happened. Anyway it didn't work out."

"Or you didn't want it to work out," Kay said, sitting beside Tina on one of the small but comfortable overstuffed chairs that added a necessary touch of hominess to her otherwise elegant office.

Defensively, Tina shook her head. "No, that's not it at all. Adam and I are just too different."

Kay had to agree. "You opted out of life in the fast lane—and he seems to love it. Of course, things aren't always what they seem."

Tina wrinkled her nose at the cliché. "Please, Kay, save me your platitudes. I'm not in the mood for them."

Kay raised her eyebrows questioningly. Tina was
seldom sharp or defensive—unless she felt threatened.

"All right, all right," Kay soothed. "There's nothing going on between you and Adam, and he's going
to Colorado because he enjoys primitive plumbing,
sporadic electricity and subzero temperatures—and
indoors, at that! Come on, Tina; it's me, Auntie Kay,
you're talking to."

Tina smiled at that. "Adam has made it clear that
he'd like—well, a resumption of our fling, but he's
agreed to settle for friendship, so we've set up some
ground rules. It's important that we work these last
few weeks in harmony, and if Adam is willing to
abide—"

"Adam Cole follow rules?" Kay got up from her
chair and headed back to the bar. "For that I need a
real drink." She poured a liberal dash of Scotch into
a tumbler and offered Tina a drink, which was declined. Shaking her head sagely, Kay declared, "The
man must be bonkers over you. But then I always
thought so. Didn't I tell you that the day you two met?
I knew I was right."

Tina, remembering Adam's own words the night
before couldn't argue, but stubbornly she answered,
"It doesn't matter what you think or what Adam
thinks. Friendship is all I'm prepared to offer him."

"Well, I'm sorry. You've been alone too long, Tina.
No man but Adam has broken through that shield of
isolation you wrap yourself in." At Tina's look of
surprise, Kay insisted, "Yes, isolation. That damn inn
is a million miles from nowhere, and you work eighteen hours a day so you don't have time to think about
anything—or anyone."

She saw Tina's eyes suddenly glint with tears and softened her words. "Honey, Bryant has been dead for almost four years. You've turned the inn into a memorial for him. Isn't it time you let go?"

And to that Tina had no answer.

Chapter 10

Tina stretched her blue-jeaned legs toward the fire, kicked off her boots and sighed. It was fun, being a guest in her own inn, and that's just what she'd been since she and Adam arrived the night before. Two couples, one with a teenaged son, were the only guests until midweek, so even Kam and Eli were able to relax. But not Adam. Bringing his energy with him from New York, he'd helped with the cooking, chopped firewood with Kam and driven into town with Eli for supplies—all that, and they'd been at Timberline less than twenty-four hours.

When Tina had gotten off the plane in Denver with Adam by her side, neither Kam nor Eli had made a comment; instead they'd greeted her with hugs and Adam with friendly handshakes. But on the way up the mountains in the old van, Eli had sneaked a couple of looks at Tina, looks that were accompanied by a little sigh of approval and a surreptitious wink. Eli wasn't exactly subtle when it came to showing her approval.

Kam hadn't said a word, then or later. He'd taken Adam for granted, almost as if he'd expected him to come along. And except for a long and detailed football discussion, he'd treated Adam like any other guest at the inn.

Eli's enthusiasm, however, could barely be kept in check until she got Tina alone in the kitchen. There, in excited whispers, she declared that Adam looked better in person than in the gossip magazines and that she thoroughly approved of the love affair.

"What you and Kam have going is a love affair," Tina hastily corrected Eli. "Adam is my boss."

"Does that mean—"

"It certainly does," Tina said firmly. "Give him room 302. I'll take my own room."

"Tina, they aren't even on the same floor!"

"Exactly," Tina replied.

They'd all gone to bed early that first night and gotten up with the roosters, as was the habit at Timberline—even Adam. He helped cook breakfast, ate in the kitchen, consuming a prodigious meal, and then went with Kam to clear a fallen tree off one of the horse trails. Through the kitchen window, Tina watched them walk into the woods, sipped her coffee and smiled to herself. Adam fit in as if he'd lived at Timberline all his life, and he'd been accepted in the same way. She should have known. Adam Cole belonged wherever he was.

In the beginning Tina hadn't believed that Adam would make the trip with her. She'd been sure that at the last minute he'd change his mind, come up with an excuse or plead a business conflict, but she couldn't have been more wrong. He'd come with her, and he'd worked diligently at the chores and joined good-naturedly in the activities.

After a pointed aside the first morning about his cold and empty bed, Adam had gotten right into the spirit of things. Kam had pretended not to hear a double meaning in the comment, which caused Eli to suppress a giggle. But Tina had come up with a quick retort of her own, offering to warm some bricks for him before bedtime. After that, Adam had made no more remarks, but he'd managed to give Tina's bottom an affectionate pat in front of Kam and Eli—to keep them guessing about the relationship.

As for Tina, she wasn't surprised at anything he said or did. This was Adam in a new setting, and he was going to take a little getting used to. In the first place, he looked different. Gone were the silk shirts and custom-made suits and hand-tooled shoes. Instead, Adam dressed in faded jeans, scuffed cowboy boots and an out-of-shape sweater over a plaid wool shirt. She couldn't imagine where he'd gotten the clothes, especially the well-worn boots; finally she decided he'd either borrowed them or paid someone to "distress" them the way dealers treated furniture to achieve an antique look. Well, he'd achieved a mountain look and he wore it well.

Adam had joined Kam and the guests for a tour of Central City, an old gold-mining town, in the afternoon, returning with enormous appetites and hair-raising tales of their venture into an abandoned mine. Still going strong after dinner, he regaled everyone with folk songs from the Pennsylvania steel mills while Kam expertly picked out the melodies on his guitar and the guests listened with no less amazement and admiration than Tina. This was something they hadn't counted on when they'd arrived at Timberline—a celebrity as entertainer.

Finally everyone went upstairs to bed but Tina, who lounged in the den over a cup of coffee, and Adam, who sat across from her by the fire reading a book about the early stagecoach routes in Colorado. She'd expected him to give it about five minutes' attention, but half an hour passed and he hadn't looked up.

As she watched him, Tina put away for good the nagging doubts she'd brought with her about his motives. In spite of his determination that she return to New York to finish the Generations shooting, Adam hadn't followed her to Colorado to watch over her. He knew as well as Tina that she had to finish the contract for more than one reason: she needed the money for the ever-demanding inn, but she also needed the self-esteem and sense of accomplishment that would come when the job was completed.

Furthermore, she'd promised Adam, and she was committed to their pact of mutual trust. Adam didn't have to worry about that; he knew Tina would keep her word and return to New York. He was here because he wanted to be with her—even on her terms. He was keeping his part of the bargain, remaining warm and friendly and only briefly affectionate—and somehow expectant. Yes, that was it. Adam acted as if he were waiting...

"Tomorrow," he said suddenly, breaking through Tina's reverie, "let's take a moonlight ride along the old stagecoach trail. Says here that the trails are particularly impressive at night—" he searched for the exact words in his book "—'when there's an eerie feeling of excitement that almost takes you back to the 1860s.'"

Tina laughed.

"That's what it says," he insisted. "Some of the old trails literally hung on the side of the mountains, where now there's just room for a horse to make his way."

Tina listened to the last bit of travelogue nonsense with interest and then inquired, "Adam, can you ride a horse?"

"Well, I'm sure I can. Yes."

"Let me put it another way. Have you ever ridden a horse?"

"Actually—no, but at night, who'll be able to tell?" He looked at her with an ingenuous grin.

"The horse, that's who," Tina said with another laugh.

They had their moonlight ride the next night. Tina roped a palomino gelding from the inn's little herd and gave Adam her mare, Mountain Dew, who knew every inch of the trail.

"All you have to do is sit up there," Kam promised as he tightened the mare's girth, "and she'll do all the rest. Think of it as riding on the back of someone's motorcycle and don't lean left or right. Just hold on and follow Tina. She's an expert horsewoman," Kam added. Not possessing any male-chauvinist traits himself, Kam wasn't aware of Adam's reaction, but Tina could see it, even in the dark.

After Kam gave both horses a smack on the rump and started them off, Tina called over her shoulder to Adam, "I'm sure with a little practice you'll be an expert, too."

Adam, concentrating on holding himself upright in the saddle, reminded her not to be condescending. At that, she dug her heels into the palomino's flanks and put him into a trot. With a silent curse and a lunge forward, Adam managed to follow.

They were wearing layers of lightweight clothing under their down jackets for protection against the bitter night cold. "At least if I fall off, all these clothes will cushion me," Adam said as he reached up with one hand and pulled his wool cap further down over his ears.

They followed the same trail that Tina had ridden that day in the early fall when she decided to return to New York. The pine woods were thick, and the path that had once been a stagecoach road was wide enough for them to ride beside each other, their legs touching occasionally as the horses picked their way along. The silence of the woods was broken by the horses' heavy breathing in the cold night air, the jingle of the bridle bits, the squeak of the leather saddles and the soft clop of hooves in the snow. These were the sounds that Tina was used to and loved; to Adam, they were new, unfamiliar and peaceful. He relaxed in the saddle and gave himself to the peace, knowing that he'd never experienced anything like it before.

They stopped at Tina's favorite overlook, dismounted—Adam with difficulty—and stood on the rock ledge even though they could see only the dim outline of the snow-covered continental divide in the distance. The palomino stomped impatiently a few times, then decided to accept his fate and began pawing in the snow in hopes of finding a blade of grass or an edible twig. Tina leaned against the horse's stout shoulder, one hand thrown over his mane. Adam dropped Mountain Dew's reins and walked over to Tina.

"Thanks for this," he said, his words making a frosty pattern in the air. "I'd kiss you, but I know the rules. Besides, my lips are frozen."

Tina laughed and looked up at him, or what she could see of him beneath the wool cap and above the down jacket. His cheeks were bright, and his eyes were sparkling. All at once, Tina wished there weren't any rules.

She started to speak, but Adam's words were first. "This is a fantastic place." He took a deep breath of crisp air and looked out over the view.

"This is my favorite spot," she told him. "I'll have to bring you here in the sunlight."

"Or in warmer weather," he suggested, "when we can see each other as well as the view. Right now, all I see of you is a red jacket and a red nose. In the summer..." he suggested.

"In the summer," Tina repeated. As they mounted and headed back toward Timberline Inn, Tina's thoughts were on a time when both the winter—and Generations—would be over.

Back at the ranch, they unsaddled the horses, and Adam led them into their stalls. Using the pitchfork as Kam had taught him that afternoon, Adam tossed a partial bale of hay to the horses. "I'll be a regular cowpoke soon," he said. It was the first time he'd spoken since the mention of summer, and there was still a kind of poignancy in the air as he put his arm around Tina and they walked up the path toward the back of the inn. The front doors were locked for the night, and the only lights on the first floor were in the kitchen, where Eli and Kam were setting up for the morning meal. Tina paused for a moment to look up at the big old house with the kitchen lights spilling out across the snow.

"It looks like a postcard," Adam commented.

Tina smiled. "To those of you who live in New York. To us, it looks like a comfortable old barn," she said. "But it's home." Tina tried to find comfort in the words as she climbed the steps to the kitchen door with Adam right behind her.

Just as she reached for the knob, the door was pulled open. "Well, it's about time you two got back." Kam stood in the doorway, arms akimbo, blocking the view behind. "We were about to send out a search party."

"We stopped at the overlook—" Tina began to explain as she stepped into the kitchen, but she didn't finish her sentence. With a great flourish Kam moved aside as he and Eli, joined quickly by Adam, broke into a rousing version of "Happy Birthday," pulling Tina into the kitchen, which had been decorated with balloons and crepe-paper streamers. Stretched across the room, from the handle on the refrigerator to the knob on the broom closet, was an eight-foot hand-painted banner declaring, "Happy Birthday, Tina!"

"Good Lord," she managed to mumble.

"Don't tell us you forgot," Adam said.

"Actually, I tried to, but I must admit I thought about it when I woke up this morning."

"And decided not to mention it," Eli chastised. As Kam opened a bottle of champagne and filled four glasses, she added, "Well, I didn't forget, Tina. I've been looking forward to this."

They all reached for a glass and toasted, "To Tina at thirty-six."

Tina moaned, and Adam added his own toast, "Beautiful at any age."

While Tina and Adam peeled off their layers of outer garments, Kam told them, "We decided to have the party here in the kitchen because it's faraway from the guests, in case they want to sleep, and because there's room for dancing."

"Dancing?" Tina wondered aloud as she piled her coat and sweaters on a chair.

"Of course. I brought in the stereo from the living room."

Adam looked at Tina and winked. Unwittingly, Kam had broken one of her rules—no dancing with Adam.

Kam, missing the byplay, put on a record and stood back, waiting for the beat. When it came, the loud cadence of a popular rock song, he grabbed Tina and began a most peculiar dance step, which she attempted to follow.

"Is this really how they dance to rock music?" she called out.

"Who knows?" Adam responded, taking Eli's hand and joining the others in the middle of the kitchen floor. "But I'll try anything. How about you, Eli?"

"Lead on," she agreed, after downing the rest of her champagne.

One hour, two rock albums and another bottle of champagne later, they all collapsed at the kitchen table. "But the celebration's not over yet," Kam reminded them as he got up and headed for the refrigerator, which he couldn't open without untying the banner. "Whoops," he said, "I didn't think of that." He tied the loose end to the freezer door. "We won't be needing that tonight. But this we need—" He turned around to reveal a huge three-layered chocolate birthday cake bedecked with bright red candles.

"Kam—" Tina couldn't believe her eyes.

"It's chocolate mousse," he offered. "Your favorite."

"It must have taken hours to make."

"About eight actually, since I had to work in stages whenever we could get you out of the kitchen. But," he added, carefully placing the tray on the kitchen table and brandishing a cake knife, "since you always nix presents on your birthday, we *had* to have a cake."

"It's . . . it's colossal," Tina declared for want of a better word.

"And why not?" he answered as Eli lit the candles. "To welcome you home."

Tina let the remark slide. They all knew she wasn't home yet. She made a silent wish before blowing out the candles, a wish that had more of Adam than Tina in it.

After Adam filled their glasses with the last drops of champagne, he offered another toast. "To Tina." This time, just before she took a sip, he leaned over and kissed her lips lightly. "Beautiful at *all* ages."

Tina felt a sudden constriction in her throat as if she were going to cry. Tears stung her eyes, and she tried to blink them back. "Why in the world am I crying?" she asked the other three.

"Because," Kam answered, "you're a crazy New York model."

But Tina knew it was because her emotions were so mixed. She was happy to be back at Timberline, happy to be with Kam and Eli again, but she wasn't sure how she'd feel when she was really home for good—without Adam.

"Just have some cake and everything'll be okay," Kam promised as Tina's fork cut into the rich chocolate. She took the first bite, and they all waited for her judgment.

Looking heavenward, Tina declared, "Fit for the gods." Eli and Adam, after enormous bites, agreed, and Kam beamed.

The evening wound down to easy music—Sinatra serenading them as they slow-danced, not trading partners this time. The sensuous flow of the music, the pressure of Adam's body against hers, the feel of his arms around her, all made Tina remember the first night that she and Adam had danced.

She had been frightened of him then—of his masculinity, his mystique, the power that he exerted over her. Adam had been at his most seductive that night, holding her much too close, using his body like a weapon to break through the barrier of her coolness. Tonight was different. He held her almost tenderly, sometimes singing aloud with the record, seemingly lost in the magic of the music. He was playing strictly by the rules.

At midnight, Kam and Eli, sleepily hand in hand, made their ways upstairs after a final kiss for Tina. She watched them leave, decided they were overdoing the sleepy look and caught Eli's eye to see if the ending, like the rest of the evening, had been planned. Tina saw a twinkle there, but she couldn't tell if it was caused by Eli's romantic notions or just too much champagne.

"And now for my present," Adam said after they'd left.

"Present?"

"The no-gift rule is for Timberline staff only. I'm a guest here." He disappeared briefly and returned with a large box.

Seeing it, Tina felt her spirits fall. She was sure that the gift was a fur coat or something else equally expensive and ostentatious to dazzle her and outdo the simplicity of the evening. That was Adam's style; he couldn't help it any more than the snow could help falling in winter. But still she was disappointed.

"This party must have been planned for days," Tina commented as she struggled with the ribbons.

"No, just this morning," he informed her.

Tina stopped to look at Adam. He'd sat down on a kitchen chair and tilted back on two of its spindly legs, watching. "Then when did you buy my present?" she wondered out loud. "You didn't leave the ranch all day."

"I bought it before we came. Your birthdate was on the Generations contract, and I make it a point to remember things that are important to me." Then he grinned sheepishly. "Besides, I have a photographic memory, or didn't I tell you that?"

"No, you didn't, but I'm not surprised." Pulling off the last of the ribbons and paper, Tina joked, "It's too small for a new furnace."

"And too large for a bread box," Adam added.

Tina lifted the top, rummaged around in the tissue paper and found the present buried beneath. This time she couldn't stop the tears as she held up the small box within the larger one—a leather-bound set of the complete works of the Brontës. They were first editions, very old and certainly rare but in perfect condition. Tina took a book from the set and opened it, delighting in the touch of the fine paper as she turned the pages. Happiness radiating from her face, she asked Adam, "Where in the world did you—"

"It wasn't that easy," Adam admitted. "I called every collector in New York and a couple in London. Finally located this set in Philadelphia. I brought it in my suitcase on the plane, wrapped in my down jacket."

"I've never been more surprised," Tina said, pulling up a chair beside him and turning to the frontispiece of another book. She felt ashamed of her earlier thoughts; again she'd been wrong about Adam Cole.

Adam took the book from her hand and examined it. "Forrester isn't the only rare-book buff in the world or the only literary...well, I was going to say scholar," Adam said with a laugh.

There was something so boyishly competitive in Adam's face that Tina couldn't stop herself. She leaned forward and kissed him, her lips closing on his for a long intoxicating moment. Tina, the one who'd made the rules of their newly established "friendship," wasn't abiding by them herself, but she didn't care. She was so touched by Adam's thoughtfulness that no other gesture seemed fitting.

When she moved away from him, he didn't pursue her with another kiss. The gesture had been hers, and he'd taken it as she'd meant it—in friendship. Yet something was churning inside of Tina, an emotion that had nothing to do with friendship. She didn't share her feelings with Adam, and if he noticed he said nothing. Still, as they rinsed the plates and loaded the dishwasher, there was a tenseness in the air between them that hadn't been present earlier. They worked quietly, their hands touching occasionally, their eyes meeting and holding until she looked away.

Finished, Tina paused in the kitchen door, her hand on the light switch. "Let's leave up the sign," Tina said.

"Sure," Adam agreed. "Until your next birthday." For some reason the tears welled in her eyes again as he put his arm around her waist and they went through the house to the front stairs.

Tina's room was on the second floor at the end of the hall. The house was quiet. No lights shone under the doors as they walked along the worn carpet toward her room.

When they reached her room, Adam left his arm around her and with his other hand gently touched her face. She leaned back against the door, not quite ready to open it and go inside. Seeing her hesitate, Adam rested his arm against the doorjamb and looked down at her.

"Happy birthday," he said softly. "Thanks for letting me be a part of your celebration."

"And thank *you* for the wonderful present."

"Surprised, aren't you?"

"About a lot of things," Tina admitted.

Adam dropped his arm from the doorway and caught her in it, enclosing her slim body and pulling her close. When he kissed her, it was a kiss more gentle than she'd expected. She felt herself clinging to him anyway as if the kiss had been one of passion—and wishing that it had been. He held his cheek against her face, and she felt a growing excitement in the coarseness of his day's growth of beard against her skin. Tina could feel his breath against her cheek, and she began to melt into him.

That's when Adam drew away, looking down at her with serious brown eyes as he spoke. "This may surprise you, too, but I'm going to respect our agreement, Tina. I'm going to walk away from you now, leave you here and go upstairs to my room."

Tina's eyes mirrored her mixed emotions. Adam could see disappointment mingled with surprise, both stronger feelings than the once-stalwart determination.

"This isn't what I want," he said softly. "I want *you*, but I made a promise, Tina, so I'm going to walk away. The rest will have to be up to you." He took a step back, his eyes locked on hers, his fingers touching her arm. "I've always been the pursuer—from the very beginning. Now you'll have to come to me." His fingers trailed down her arm and grasped her hand for an instant before he turned and walked away.

Tina watched him walk to the end of the hall and up the staircase to the third floor. Then she opened her door and went into the room. Kam had stopped by and lit the fire, but the warmth she felt was the warmth left over from Adam's strong arms and gentle lips, and it blended with the remembrance of another night when they'd been together, when he hadn't left her at the door. Adam had come to her that night; now he was asking that she come to him.

Tina sat down on the bed and pulled off her boots. Then she took off her sweater and pulled the shirttail of her plaid shirt out of her jeans and lay back on the bed, her memories of need mixed with more recent memories of companionship. She'd gotten to know Adam during these days in Colorado, to know him as a man who not only fired her need but touched her heart.

She thought about him sitting at the kitchen table over a cup of hot tea while Eli made out the grocery list and then helping Eli clear the dishes after the guests had finished their breakfast. She remembered standing at the kitchen window while Adam and Kam chopped wood for the fireplace before heading for the barn to feed the horses. With a smile, she remembered Adam on horseback—uneasy at first but willing to venture into the unknown. He'd been so different here at Timberline. In her milieu, where they were both relaxed and easy, he'd made no demands on her. Now it was time for Tina's decision, and it wouldn't be an easy one. Her need for Adam was great, but was it greater than her dread of heartbreak?

Tina realized that she knew the answer. Her feelings for him had grown stronger since they'd been at Timberline, and now they were strong enough to name. The name was love. She loved him, and no matter the future or the hurt, she couldn't deny that love. It was stronger than all the rest.

Tina got off the bed and stood in front of the full-length mirror to examine what she saw there. What she saw was a woman whose eyes were inky dark with need, whose body ached to be held. What she couldn't see but could only feel was the pounding rhythm inside that was her racing heart.

She could hear the pounding; it was the only sound in the quiet room. Somewhere outside, far in the distance, a coyote barked and then was silent, and once more there was only the pounding of her heart. Upstairs, Adam waited, but the waiting was almost over; Tina was going to him.

She didn't stop to put her sweater back on or even to step into her slippers but went out into the hall and on soundless bare feet hurried up the stairs to Adam's room.

He was already in bed. The fire dwindling in the grate gave the room a shadowy and mysterious feeling, and as Tina stepped inside the door, she was unsure for a moment if she'd made the right decision. She couldn't see the expression on Adam's face; she didn't know what he was feeling. Hesitating, she stood in the shadows.

Adam said nothing; he just held out his arms to her. Before Tina put her hand in his, she pulled off her jeans, unbuttoned her shirt and dropped it to the floor. Shivering in the cold, she was warmed the instant her hand touched his.

Adam pulled back the covers so she could slide into the bed beside him, and then she saw the look in his eyes. It was a look so intense it melted her heart as his kiss warmed her bones and her body infused her once-cool flesh with its heat.

"Tina," he whispered as he kissed her cheeks and forehead, holding her face in both hands and smoothing back her hair that was still a little disheveled from hours before when she'd pulled off her wool cap and shaken it free. "Tina," he said again softly, wonderingly.

"Didn't you know I'd come to you?" she asked as she returned his greedy kisses.

"I had no idea what you'd do. I never know." His voice had hoarseness in it, an aching need, but there was also relief now that he was holding her in his arms. "I've been waiting so long to feel you like this again, to touch you," he said as his hands roamed her now warm body.

His fingers found her breast, her nipple taut not with the chill of the air but with expectation and excitement. He was gentle now, teasing the pink rosebud of her nipple, rolling it lightly between his fingers. Deep inside, Tina felt a warm delicious wave of desire begin to flow through her veins and muscles, all the fibers of her body, yielding to the man beside her.

Outside in the night, the coyote barked again, and inside, just across the room, the last vestiges of the fire crackled and sparked. Tina heard nothing but her own quickened breathing and the pounding acceleration of her heart as her need increased, the need to become one with Adam and experience every sensation through him.

His lips nuzzled her cheek, her ear, her neck. "I want to taste you all over. I want to feel my mouth on your breasts, Tina."

Just the thoughts of what he suggested made her skin tingle, and when Adam threw back the covers, his lips created a trail of fire across her skin, a sensation that was more than she'd anticipated, more than she'd remembered. She felt the whisper of whiskers against the smoothness of her skin; she felt his warm, moist mouth suckling the fullness of her breast, and such an unnameable pleasure coursed through her that Tina shut her eyes and let a low moan of joy escape from her lips.

Not yet satisfied with his feast on her breasts but hungry for more of her, Adam's lips slid across her rib cage, his tongue leaving a moist pattern on her skin. He kissed the indentation of her waist and then nibbled along the line of her hip bone. Finally, he found the aching sweetness between her thighs.

Involuntarily, Tina's back arched when she felt his mouth on her, and she shuddered with delirious release as paroxysms of pleasure cascaded through her. When the sensation ended, she fell back on the bed, thinking that nothing more could happen to her, that such pleasure couldn't be duplicated. But Adam's hands began their magic once again, cupping her breasts, rubbing his palms against her deliciously swollen nipples. His hands singed her tender skin, and Tina knew that her need could again be as powerful as it had been when she first stepped into his room.

Tina could hear Adam whispering to her, speaking words of affection and desire. "I want you so much, Tina. I want everything to be perfect for you... always."

"I want you, too, Adam, more than I've ever wanted a man. More than I've ever needed anyone."

She kissed him, insinuating her tongue into the silkiness of his mouth, pressing her breasts against his chest.

When they'd made love that first time, Tina had been shy, a stranger to the mysteries of his body and the wonders of his lovemaking. Adam, too, had not been so bold and seeking as tonight. But now they were both ready to fulfill each other's every need. As Tina lay in Adam's arms, her hand stole along the line of his back, across his lean hip until she found and caressed his male hardness. There was no hesitation in her touch, no tentativeness, only a feverish urgency to let her hand work magic. And it did. He grew for her, nearer and nearer the peak of his desire until his need equaled hers. Tina rose on her knees, and as Adam turned over, she slipped on top of him.

Slowly she let herself down on his shaft of masculine desire, as eager to welcome him as Adam was to enter her, smoothly, filling her, joining with her, melting into her. This, she thought, *this* is what she'd waited for, yearned for. Their first time had been an act of passion; this was an act of binding love, for she did love him; she'd admitted that to herself and now she was showing Adam her love in the most natural and beautiful way imaginable—by giving herself to him.

Tina's hands gripped his shoulders, which were slippery with perspiration, and she felt the muscles and sinews of his arms, which had held her with such strength, such gentleness. At the place where their bodies joined, Adam filled her so completely that she wanted to hold him there forever, never to be without him again. Tina could see Adam's face, his eyes shining with passion for her as she moved in time to their ecstatic union. As the passion gathered force, she leaned away from him, but he caught her wrists and then grasped her hands when her wrists slipped away. She flung her head back, giving herself to the man she loved at the same moment that he gave himself to her.

When the last tremors of release had left them, when their heartbeats became less frantic and their breathing less labored, Adam pulled the covers over them, and Tina curled up in his arms. They burrowed under the downy quilt like survivors in a warm cave. Tina rested her head in a hollow that seemed created just for her—where his shoulder and arm joined—and he rested his chin against the top of her head and wrapped his legs around her.

"No more platonic rules, ever again," Adam said with a smile in his voice. "Not after the way you gave yourself to me tonight."

"I was wanton, wasn't I?" she asked without the least trace of embarrassment.

"Wonderfully wanton," he agreed, pulling her even closer. "And do you know something? I don't ever want to lose you."

"I don't think you will," Tina said softly, and somehow a commitment was made between them, one that surprised her, one that she hadn't thought they were ready for. She wasn't sure where it would lead, but she was ready to begin her journey. They would talk about it again before they left Colorado; Tina felt sure of that. For tonight, these few words were enough. Content, Tina snuggled closer.

"I'm not even sleepy," Adam said. "Kam worked me like a slave all day, and you took me on that long ride—"

"Both were your ideas," Tina reminded him.

"And now it's after midnight, and I feel like talking and laughing and holding on to you until morning. I've never felt this way before. It's never been like this for me—afterward," he added, kissing the top of her head.

"Never, Adam?" Tina asked, for she, too, had experienced never-before feelings with him tonight.

"No," he admitted. "Certainly not with the women I've known since my marriage; not even with Pam. Only with you." He put his hand under her chin and lifted it enough so that he could kiss her mouth. "Only with you."

After the kiss, Tina snuggled against him, her head tracing an idle pattern along the smooth muscle of his arm. "What happened, Adam?" she said cautiously. "With you and Pam and your marriage?" She'd heard about Pam from Holly, but she wanted to hear from Adam, and she thought that now, since he had mentioned Pam's name, he might be ready to talk.

There was no hesitation in his answer. "We grew apart," he said simply. "That often happens. The early years were easy because we both had everything we wanted. After I had to give up football, our lives changed. I suppose that's when a marriage is tested, when it comes on difficult times. Ours didn't stand the test. Now I wonder how much was there in the beginning."

Adam's hands drifted through her hair. "I don't believe it was ever like this," he said, and then corrected himself. "I know it wasn't."

Tina realized what he meant, for she, too, was feeling it now—a different kind of passion followed by a different kind of peace.

"I'd been successful," Adam went on, "and I wanted to stay that way. Hell, I was driven; let's face it. After I bought Century, I threw myself into the work, and often there was no time for Pam. She wanted to share the success, but she didn't want me to work so hard for it. I guess she envisioned that it would be like pro football—three hours on Sunday." Adam laughed. "But I gave my job twelve hours a day, seven days a week. If I had it to do over, I hope I'd be mature enough to find a middle ground."

"We can't relive the past," Tina said.

"No, but I don't want to make the same mistake again." That was Adam's commitment to himself— not to repeat the past. Lying in his arms, listening to him talk, Tina felt a part of that commitment.

"Pam had a bad case of wanderlust," Adam continued, "and the farther she got away from home, the more often she was unfaithful to me. I think a lot of the blame is mine, because I might have been able to prevent what happened. I remember exactly when it began. She wanted me to fly to Cannes with her for the film festival. We had an invitation to stay on a friend's yacht, but I was too busy, couldn't get away. Hell, I can't really blame her. She needed love and attention. She'd had it all her life, and then I wasn't there to give it to her."

Tina remembered her own marriage to Bryant. They'd both sacrificed so much for each other— maybe too much, she thought. "Even if you could start over, could you give up your work, Adam?"

He thought for a while before he answered. "No, but I could be more flexible, less driven. Look at the time I've taken to be with you even in the midst of my company's most important campaign. I could never have done that ten years ago. Maybe I wanted the marriage to be over. No," he corrected himself emphatically. "I didn't want that—because of Holly. When Pam finally left and wanted to take Holly with her, I couldn't let my daughter go. I couldn't give her up."

"She's not a possession," Tina reminded him.

"No, but she's a part of me, and I needed her. I believe she needed me, too, at that time. It wasn't Pam's infidelity that made me fight for my daughter. Hell, I wasn't in a position to condemn her for that. It was her wanderlust. She couldn't have given Holly the consistency a little girl needs. Pam was always on the move from one country to the next—villa to chateau to hotel to yacht. My base is New York. Holly knows where home is."

"But no visits . . ."

"Let's just say that my ex-wife has a short attention span. When Holly was younger, Pam would make arrangements to visit and then call and cancel. I finally stopped telling Holly about the plans, since her mother seldom followed through. They were most apt to see each other on the spur of the moment—if their paths just happened to meet."

Tina remembered the visit in Italy that Holly had mentioned.

"Long ago, I asked Pam not to contact Holly directly," Adam said, "because whenever she did, the child only got set up for another disappointment. But being so young, Holly got the wrong idea, I'm afraid, and thought I was keeping them apart. It wasn't really like that, but I'm beginning to realize now that it was difficult for both of them."

Tina was realizing, too, that the picture of Pam she'd gotten through Holly's eyes was not a complete one. She'd known at the time that Holly's was only one version, and she was grateful that Adam was allowing her to see another picture, one that included his feelings.

Adam moved slightly, and when Tina looked up at him, she saw the shadow of a frown. "Recently, Holly has been dropping her mother's name more and more into her conversations," he said. "I think she wants to get my reaction. I also think something is going on."

Tina felt her heartbeat accelerate. She wouldn't betray her conversation with Holly, but as she thought of the girl's shining face when she'd mentioned the phone call to her mother, Tina could only hope that Holly hadn't been set up for yet another disappointment.

"You're awfully quiet," Adam said, moving his hand along Tina's back.

"Sleepy," she told him, but she wasn't really sleepy. She was worried, and she didn't know how to tell Adam about her concerns.

"I suppose we should get to sleep," he suggested, "especially since Kam will get me up at daybreak with a whole list of morning chores." He turned Tina in his arms until her back was against him, fitting perfectly. Like two spoons in a drawer, they snuggled comfortably into the curves of each other's body. Adam drifted immediately to sleep.

Tina had a more difficult time sleeping, and it seemed as if only moments had passed when her fitful dreams were interrupted by a loud, insistent pounding on the door. Kam's voice punctuated the bangs.

"Adam, there's a phone call for you. Some woman who sounds hysterical. I told her you'd be right down."

Muttering curses under his breath, Adam crawled out of the warm cocoon of the bed and pulled on his clothes. After he left, Tina remained huddled beneath the tangled covers. The early-morning phone call was somehow ominous, and she couldn't shake her feelings of dread.

Ten minutes later Adam came back in the room, a look of desperation written on his face. "That was Mrs. Dale," he said in a strangled voice. "Pam's back in New York, and Holly's run away to her."

Chapter 11

Adam was silent for the first hour of the plane trip back to New York, locked in his own thoughts. Tina made no attempt to bring him out of his reverie, hoping that soon he would open his thoughts to her. Finally he did.

When the stewardess came by with the drink cart, Adam spoke for the first time, ordering for Tina and himself in a familiar way that told the flight attendant he and Tina belonged together. It was a familiarity that pleased Tina, even surprised her, especially after the long silence. His next words pleased her more.

"Thanks, Tina," he said, turning to look at her with tired eyes. "Thanks for coming back with me." He took her hand, and some of the sadness seemed to melt away and become absorbed by her. She was proud that she had the strength to help and understand.

She held on tightly to his hand. "I'm also concerned for Holly," she said.

"I know you are," Adam answered almost thankfully.

"She wants to make the right decision for herself."

"But not for me..."

"Of course, for you, too, Adam," she disagreed. "But the decision must ultimately be for Holly."

"Well, she damn well isn't making the right one by choosing to go with her mother—not for me, not for Pam and most certainly not for Holly," Adam said angrily.

Tina, not expecting the outburst, was silent. Soon Adam's anger dissipated and he began to talk quietly. As he spoke, he held Tina's hand in a manner that seemed detached but brought them closer, Tina thought, than ever before. While looking away from her, staring out the window into the clouds, Adam sensed her presence keenly and was glad for her strength.

He talked about the past, about Holly as a child, and Tina began to realize that even if he'd been an often absent father, he'd also been a caring one. Adam recalled incidents, little moments in his daughter's life, that many fathers would have forgotten or not even noticed at all. He remembered the first words she spoke and the first complete sentence.

"The day she put a few words together into a sentence nearly bowled me over," he admitted proudly. "Holly was standing at the window of our house in Erie. It was a snowy day. I'd been at football practice, and she watched me come up the walk and into the house, shaking the snow from my slicker." He smiled to himself as he remembered. "I put my coat in the closet and went into the living room just as she turned away from the window and said, 'Here's me, Daddy.'"

Tina heard the catch in Adam's throat, and she made herself look away for a moment so he could compose himself. When he continued, his voice was steady. "I was really proud of her. I've been proud often since then, but I'm not sure I ever told her. I'm not even sure I told her that day." He added with brutal honesty, "Just as often I've been annoyed with Holly, and *that* I always told her."

"Lots of parents make that mistake," Tina assured him. She knew it was true but wasn't sure it was particularly comforting or even very meaningful since she wasn't a parent herself.

Adam talked on about his daughter and about his ex-wife and her series of failed attempts to see Holly over the years. By the time the plane began its approach into New York, he was facing what had happened and offering himself alternatives.

"Maybe I should let her try this—living with her mother. Maybe she has to get it out of her system." He paused just long enough to reconsider. "It won't work," he assured Tina, "but maybe it's inevitable." Then he drew up a deep breath and changed his mind. "I can't let her do it," he said. "Not yet."

Tina wasn't sure he could stop Holly, and the expression on her face must have revealed that doubt, for he reminded her quickly, "I have custody, Tina. I can refuse to let her go."

"Yes," Tina said quietly.

"And I will—for now. Holly isn't prepared for this offer of Pam's. She's never given a moment's thought to living abroad. Now the chance to go with Pam is sprung on her out of the blue. It's too quick," he reiterated. "She needs time to think about it—away from Pam's sphere of influence. It's an appealing offer, but I doubt if the reality of living with Pam—living like a damned gypsy—will be appealing at all."

Tina still held his hand without responding. It wasn't her place to contribute to Adam's thoughts—and that's all they were. He was thinking aloud, using her as a sounding board. He was glad to have her there, but he wanted nothing from her except a sympathetic ear.

"Holly needs to finish school." Adam was aware that this was his only legitimate reason to keep his daughter with him.

"And the campaign."

"I don't give a damn about the campaign," he shot back, and Tina realized that was true. He was thinking only of Holly. Tina was thinking of her, too, and of their conversation that had precipitated Holly's first phone call to her mother. Tina remembered that day when she had told Holly to listen to her heart, and she wondered if the remark had been too pat, too easy. There was more involved, Tina knew, than just flying off on the wings of newfound love for her mother, hoping they would be strong enough to keep her in the air. But as Adam had wisely said, the reality might not be anything like the dream.

Tina went with Adam to his apartment. It seemed to be understood that she would stay with him through this ordeal, sharing a closeness different from the days at Timberline, stronger because so many emotions were involved. He was taking her into his life now, not just into his bed—although they would share that, too, Tina realized, but not yet. That would come later after he'd seen his daughter.

"Has she come back?" Adam asked Mrs. Dale as they stepped into the apartment.

The housekeeper, a strained look on her normally robust face, shook her head and responded in a tearful voice, "She packed up two suitcases of her prettiest clothes, called a cab and left, just like I told you on the phone. Oh, Mr. Cole, I tried to stop her; I told her she was making a mistake, but she wouldn't listen to me. With you gone, what else could I have done?" she pleaded.

"Nothing, Mrs. Dale," Adam responded kindly in spite of the pain he was feeling. "But I do have some more questions." He proceeded to bring himself up to date on every detail of the past twenty-four hours, but in fact he learned very little more. Holly had left without saying where she could be reached and without mentioning when she and her mother planned to leave New York for Europe.

Adam listened to Mrs. Dale impatiently and then told Tina, "I imagine Pam's at the Plaza. That would be the only place to suit her style. I'm going to try to see her—and Holly—after I talk to my lawyer." He turned to Mrs. Dale, who was still standing tensely in the same spot, her tears beginning to brim over behind her thick glasses. "Did you make an appointment with Ross for me?" Adam asked her.

Happy that she'd accomplished something for her beloved employer, Mrs. Dale nodded vigorously. "Mr. Ross said to come straight to his office as soon as you arrived. He said he'd make time to see you," Mrs. Dale reported with a certain amount of respectful satisfaction.

"Thanks," Adam said as he put on his coat again.

"Do you want me to come with you?" Tina asked.

Adam shook his head. "No, just stay here, Tina, if you will. I'm going to try to see both of them, and whatever happens, I'd like you to be here when I get back."

He didn't bend over to kiss her or even reach out to take her hand; yet Tina still felt the closeness. It was stronger than a touch or a kiss would have been. She tried to smile as he left.

Mrs. Dale was attempting a smile, too, but it was hopeless. Her tears were falling too fast. "I've been crying for that poor child and for Mr. Cole. Why, if Holly really tries to go off with her mother, I don't know what he'll do...."

Tina could only nod sympathetically. She wasn't sure what Adam would do, either.

"How can I help?" Mrs. Dale wondered aloud and tearfully.

Tina created a job that would keep the housekeeper busy and in another part of the apartment; the tears were beginning to be contagious. "Why don't you start getting dinner ready?" As soon as she'd made the suggestion, Tina knew that it was a good one. Adam hadn't eaten since breakfast, and returning home to a good dinner would help, no matter what happened with the lawyer, Pam or Holly. "Make some of his favorites," she suggested, adding further impetus.

Quickly, Mrs. Dale was off to the kitchen, where a task awaited her that suited her talents and Adam's needs. She was nescessary again. As for Tina, she didn't feel necessary at all. Her only job was to wait—and worry.

Tina was afraid Adam would have little luck convincing Holly to talk to him. Holly was stubborn, and when she got an idea into her head, logic wasn't at all useful in dislodging it. She needed to come to her own conclusions. But she *could* be directed; Tina knew that very well. Unintentionally, she'd directed the girl herself when she'd told Holly to listen to her heart. She'd listened all right, and now Pam was here, ready to take Holly away. However remotely, Tina had played a part in the whole scenario, and she intended to tell Adam about her conversation with Holly as soon as he returned whether he was successful in seeing his daughter or not. And Tina doubted he would be.

She was right.

"Holly refused to see me," he said as he came in the door, his coat already off. "But she'd talked to Ross this morning. He couldn't get much out of her except that she'd decided to 'listen to her heart.'" Adam dropped his coat on a chair. "Does that sound familiar, Tina?" He turned to face her, and she could see that his eyes were narrowed to slits, his forehead was furrowed and his mouth was clenched in a tight line. The grim look was all for her.

Tina nodded. "I was going to tell you about that..." she began.

"I just bet you were."

It had been a long time since Tina had heard that tone of voice. For a few marvelous days in Colorado, she'd begun to think she would never hear it again.

"Holly listened to her heart all right," Adam said sarcastically, "by calling her mother and starting this whole mess all over again."

"She would have gotten in touch with Pam eventually, Adam." Tina refused to take all the blame for what, in fact, had been inevitable from the beginning.

"May I remind you, Tina, that this was the wrong time?" Adam crossed to the bar at the far end of the room, passing right by Tina without a glance. While he fixed his drink, without offering one to her, the silence was frigid. When he finally ended it, his words were no less cold.

"You showed wonderful judgment, Tina, telling a fifteen-year-old to run her own life. My Lord, how did you think she'd interpret your words? She adores you, and you gave her permission—I can't believe you did it, the woman I lov—"

He broke off, not able to admit his feelings, which Tina could only hope weren't going to be altered by the events of the past week. Those events had moved like lightning, changing and then changing again. Just hours before, she'd lain in Adam's arms, and now he refused to look at her. She'd been wrong, Tina knew now, to involve herself in Holly's life.

"I'm sorry," was all that she could manage. "Don't you know how badly I feel?"

"Perhaps you should have thought of that before you offered advice to my daughter." Adams words were like chips of ice, colder than the Colorado snow.

"You know I'd never do anything to hurt Holly—or you," Tina defended herself. "But it's over; I can't take back my words to her."

"No, you've done your part. The rest is up to me. Ross tells me that Pam's not planning to leave for Europe until next week. Holly is going to stay with her—at the Plaza, as I suspected—until they go abroad together." Adam took two long gulps of his drink. "Legally, I have every right to have her stopped at the airport and returned to me."

"Maybe if you could just talk to her first . . ." Tina offered weakly.

"I told you, Tina. She refuses to see me."

Suddenly, Tina knew exactly what she was going to do, and it surprised even her, for she was going to interfere again. No matter what the girl decided, Adam needed a chance with her—he needed his moment. Tina remembered the first time she'd met Adam and Holly—the arrogant man and the sulky girl. Tina hadn't liked either of them then; now she loved them both, and she was sure she could get them together—at least to talk. Her decision made, Tina tried to change the subject. "Mrs. Dale fixed dinner," she offered.

"Fine," Adam answered, downing his drink and mixing another one. "Don't be hurt if I decide not to join you." The sarcasm was heavy, but Tina tried to understand and curbed her own quick retort. Adam's anger at her was compounded by his hurt and his fear about Holly.

Tina knew that she couldn't do anything tonight, not with Adam glowering at her from across the room. In the morning she'd try her plan—with Holly, not

Adam. As difficult as the girl was to reach, at this point she'd be a lot easier to get to than her father.

After a sleepless night—at her apartment, having left Adam before he had a chance to berate her further—Tina dragged herself to the health club to work up the stamina necessary for a confrontation at the Plaza.

But she didn't have to go to the hotel after all. Holly was at the gym, and Tina had the distinct impression that she wasn't there for a workout. Even though she kept her distance at first, she was there to see Tina. Neither of them admitted their need to talk as they moved together through the half-hour routine. Except for the counting, they were silent, and silently they showered, dressed and made their way into the snack bar. Finally, sipping fruit drinks, they took a table in the corner and Tina spoke up.

"Okay," she said. "Tell me about it. I want to hear everything."

Holly did her best not to let her emotions show, but the thin veneer of sophistication kept slipping. "My mom came to town a couple of days ago while you and Dad were gone. She asked me to stay with her at the Plaza and then go on to Europe."

Holly paused, as if waiting for Tina's reaction. When none came, she continued. "Mom wants me to go to France with her for Christmas and then on to Rome. I could go to school there and learn Italian."

Tina didn't remind her that she still had the semester to finish at her school in New York and her job to complete for Century Cosmetics. It wasn't her place to argue or to suggest or even set up a meeting between father and daughter. But for that she planned to overstep the boundaries again. She'd somehow been the catalyst in getting Holly together with her mother; now she wanted to use that same influence to get the girl together with her father.

"Europe could be a good experience for me," Holly went on. "Living abroad has so much to offer. Here I have only my career as a model." The words sounded as if they'd come directly from her mother's mouth. Holly sipped her drink and looked straight into Tina's eyes. "I did that for him, for my dad. I thought it would make him love me more, but it didn't work. I don't want to model anymore."

Tina remained silent, but she had the feeling that Holly was still groping. The girl hadn't made a choice yet. She knew what she didn't want, but she still wasn't sure what she wanted.

"Have you talked this over with your mother?"

"Not really," Holly admitted. "She said she wanted to take me to Europe, and I just sort of fell in with the plan. So when I packed my bags and moved over to the Plaza, I told Mrs. Dale I was going away for a long time with Mom."

"But you haven't really decided?"

"No." Holly's eyes slid away from Tina's gaze.

Tina wasn't going to help Holly make such an important decision about her life. That was up to her parents, but she could offer a suggestion, nonthreatening and casual. "Why don't you talk to your mother about it—really talk? And then discuss it with you father."

Holly shook her head. "That's not going to be easy. I've lived away from my mom all these years, and I've

never talked to her—even when we were together—
about anything important." She took another gulp
from her glass. "The funny thing is, I've lived
with Dad all my life, and I haven't talked to him,
either."

"Then it's about time."

Holly finished the drink and went to the bar for another. Her appetite never seemed to fail, Tina thought
with amazement, no matter what happened in her life.
When she returned with a tofu burger and another
drink, Holly admitted, "I can probably get Mom to
discuss all the reasons for me to go and all the reasons
for me to stay. I think she'd be fair. Maybe I could just
make up my mind after I talk to her and not have to
discuss this with Dad."

"That wouldn't be fair, Holly, no matter what the
decision. Even if you make up your mind, you still
have to tell him."

All traces of the successful, sophisticated young
model disappeared as Holly looked at Tina with
pleading blue eyes. "Will you help me, Tina?"

"I'll be there if you want me," she promised, "but
the rest will be up to you."

Two days passed with no word from Holly. Whatever her decision, it was all hers now. Tina could do
nothing more for Holly. But she could do something
for Adam. She knew he was going through hell—alone
at a time when he desperately needed someone with
him and was too proud to ask.

Tina arrived at his apartment just as Adam was
finishing his early-morning run.

"Once before, you said that I'd have to come to you," she told him as they walked together into his building. "I'm doing it again."

"Thank God you are," he said, putting his arm around her and then, when they stepped into his apartment, pulling her close. He'd perspired through his warm-up jacket, and Tina could feel the dampness against her body. She welcomed it as she welcomed the manly, musky scent of him.

"Forgive what I said the other day, Tina. I was angry... and afraid. I still am."

"Oh, Adam, Adam." In her voice so much was spoken, so much forgiven.

"I'm afraid of losing everything. You and Holly— everything that means so much to me." His arms encircled her more tightly, as if he didn't ever want to let her go.

Tina looked up at Adam and saw that his face was wet, not with sweat but with tears. She pressed her cheek against his and, feeling the salty warmth of his tears, assured him, "You're not losing me, Adam. Ever."

"What about Colorado? The inn?"

"It's just a building. A place filled with memories. You mean more to me than Timberline, Adam. You and Holly." She felt his body tense. "Has she called?" When he shook his head, Tina could feel her own tears building. "She will," Tina promised, praying that her words were true.

Adam moved away from the comfort of her arms, as if he needed to be on his own when he faced the prospect of his daughter's leaving him. "I'm not so good at talking to Holly. I've given her a lot of orders

over the years, but I've never really talked to her."
Adam dropped onto the sofa, admitting what Holly
had already told Tina.

"Then start now. Tell her everything you've wanted
to tell her from the beginning—from that day when
she said, 'Here's me, Daddy.' Let her know how you
feel. Show her the man who loves his daughter so
much he can cry over losing her."

Adam's face closed then, and his lips tightened, but
Tina was determined to break through the barrier. She
sat beside him and took his hand. "Oh, Adam, don't
try to hide your feelings. You're a very strong man,
but you've never been more of a man than when you
let me see the tears."

She reached for him, and he closed his arms around
her with such need that Tina felt in holding him she
was holding all of his emotions from his love through
his fear, touching his soul. She held tight and hoped—
for Adam, for Holly and for herself.

Holly didn't call; she just showed up. Adam and
Tina had finished dinner at a table drawn up to the
fireplace, suffering through Mrs. Dale's dour looks
and doleful smiles until finally the housekeeper cleared
away the dishes and took her despondency into the
kitchen for good.

But Adam still held on to his despair as he pushed
aside his third cup of coffee, stood up and began to
pace. "Maybe I should go to the hotel. Just get Holly
and take her the hell out of there. That's what I should
do," he decided. "Go and get her."

Adam knew that wasn't a solution, and so did Tina.
"If you do that, you'll be together, but you won't be

happy and you'll ruin any chance for honest communication—ever. Wait for her, Adam. I know she'll come. Just be patient."

Adam almost smiled. "That's not one of my virtues."

"Holly will be here," Tina repeated. "But she needs to make this decision herself."

"Just like her decision to call her mother?" Adam directed a frown at Tina.

"Don't glower at me, Adam. That call had been coming for a long time. She's not a baby; someday you'll have to let Holly grow up."

Adam was just about to answer when they heard a key in the lock. Holly walked into the living room. She was wearing jeans and a down jacket; her face was devoid of makeup, and her hair had been whipped around her face and shoulders by the autumn wind. She looked young and very vulnerable. Tentatively, Adam stood up.

Just as tentatively, as if expecting anger from her father, Holly said, "We have to talk."

The look she'd expected wasn't angry at all but welcoming. "I know, baby," he answered.

Holly smiled weakly at Tina and sat down in a chair beside the sofa. "I had to see Mom," she said. "I had to find out how we felt about each other."

Adam nodded silently, understandingly.

"But I never could have done it without Tina. I never could have called my mom." Holly took a deep, trembling breath. "Tina told me to listen to my heart, so I did. I found out that my mother likes me—"

"Likes you?" Adam interrupted. "Why shouldn't she, since you're such a likable girl? Haven't I lived with you for fifteen years? Don't I know?"

Holly was very serious when she answered. "I'm not sure you do."

Adam's face became as solemn as his daughter's. "Then tell me, please."

Silently, Tina watched father and daughter, becoming an audience for them as, like players reading their parts for the first time, they hesitantly spoke their lines, beginning with Holly.

"I've gotten to know Mom in the past few days," she said. "And I like her." The last was added a bit defiantly.

Adam's answer was soft. "I'm glad."

"But I don't know whether or not I'm ready to share her life-style."

Tina could see the relief written all over Adam's face; she could even see it in his body, which, tense for so many days, began to relax.

"I wanted to please her just like I've always wanted to please you, but I know now that was wrong."

Adam's voice was still soft and low. "You're the one that matters, Holly. It's time to think about yourself."

"Do you really believe that?" Her blue eyes narrowed and studied her father's face as if to make sure his words were real.

"Of course." Adam reached out for his daughter's hand, but she wasn't ready yet. She made a little movement away from him before she spoke.

"All right," Holly said, "I'll tell you the rest. If I stay in New York, I don't want to model anymore."

Surprise showed on Adam's face, but Tina couldn't see any anger there.

"Oh, don't worry," Holly added quickly. "I'll finish the Generations work."

"It doesn't matter, honey."

"Yes, it does," she disagreed. "I made a commitment. But after that I'm through with modeling. I never liked it. I only did it for you."

"For me?" Adam was genuinely stunned. "I never cared about your modeling. It never meant a damn to me." There was no misreading the emotion in his voice.

"Then why didn't you tell me?" Holly's voice raised to a high tremble. "I thought you wanted me to be a success—like you."

"And I thought you worked because you loved it."

"I hated it," she cried. "All those long hours with no time for myself, no friends, no dates, no parties. Nothing but stupid fame. I'm fifteen years old, and I'm sick of fame!"

"I never knew any of that," Adam admitted.

"Because I couldn't tell you." There was anguish in her voice and the glitter of unshed tears in her eyes. "And because I couldn't ask."

"Oh, Daddy." The tears started now, coursing down her cheeks, tears of relief and reconciliation and love.

Adam stepped toward his daughter, lifted her from the chair and hugged her tightly. "You haven't called me that in years," he said.

"Not since I was a little girl," Holly snuffled against his shoulder.

Adam smiled, and his smile included Tina. She'd been part of this from the first moment, silent but there for him, and Adam had known it. So had Holly. He held his daughter at arm's length, looking at her as if for the first time. "Tell me—and Tina—what you want, Holly."

"I...I want to go to school full-time." She sat down on the sofa beside Tina, talking to her now. That was easier; it would be a while before she got used to this new communication. "I want to be like a real kid with dates and friends and pimples. And I don't even care if I get fat." Laughter mingling with her tears produced a kind of giggling hiccup. "Oh, Tina, I'm so tired of exercising!"

"Me, too," Tina said, giving her a hug. "Have you told your mom?"

"No. I had to find out what Dad thought about my quitting work, but when I tell her, I think she'll understand. She realizes that I can't move around the way she does, from place to place like a gypsy. It might be fun sometimes—like next summer, when she'll be in Greece. I'd like to visit her there. That is, if Dad approves."

She looked over at her father, but the little-girl look was gone, replaced by the sophisticated young woman. That was part of Holly now; she would never be able completely to shed her sophistication. She smiled broadly at her father, tossing her luxuriant hair.

"Dad approves," Adam said, "as long as you come back to me. To us. I can't handle losing either one of my girls again."

Holly looked at Tina. "We three are a pretty good team. Wonder what the possibilities are of making it permanent?"

"Not bad," Tina said, "if your father plays his cards right."

Holly flashed another big smile, her tears forgotten. She stood up and stretched mightily as if some great weight had been lifted from her shoulders. "Well, I'll leave that up to you two. Meanwhile, I'm going to see if Mrs. Dale has any leftovers, and then I'm climbing into bed. Mom's gone to some dinner party tonight. She'll only be in town a couple more days."

Adam nodded. "I think you should see her as much as possible."

"Thanks, Dad," Holly called over her shoulder as she headed for the kitchen.

When the door closed behind her, Adam sank down on the sofa, and Tina leaned up against him with a sigh. "What a week. I feel as though I've aged a thousand years since my birthday."

"You were right when you told me to trust my child," Adam said, kissing her forehead lightly. "You were also right when you told Holly to listen to her heart. If she hadn't had this time with Pam, Holly would never have gotten to know her mother—and I would never have gotten to know my daughter. You always seem to be right, Tina." He kissed her again, this time on the corner of her mouth. "So stay with me to keep me—and Holly—in line. And to love us," he added, this time covering her mouth with his own.

Tina's mouth opened under his, her hands threading through his hair, her lips holding his, not wanting to break the contact. Adam kissed her fully, tasting the sweet nectar of her mouth, exploring with his tongue, letting his hands glide up and down the softness of her back.

As they kissed, Tina felt all the pain and anguish of the past days flow away, leaving nothing but the hope and excitement of the days ahead. Their love had survived this, and it would survive much more and stay intact. It was strong, and it was forever. Tina had no idea what Adam had planned for them, but whatever it was, her kiss was proof that she would be here beside him. When the kiss ended, Adam told her what he had in mind, and it included more than just the days ahead; it included the years stretching toward forever.

"I want to get married right away," he whispered. "Now. Let's just do it; act first and think later."

"Isn't it a little late at night for a wedding?" Tina answered, trying to hide the heavy pounding of her heart with her light remark.

"Tomorrow, then," Adam consented.

"I need to tell you something first," Tina said, looking up at him with serious blue eyes.

"I've heard enough talk tonight," Adam argued, half teasingly. "Can't it wait?"

"Nope, it can't."

He shifted so that her head rested against his chest. His hands played sensuously along her shoulder, her neck, her breast, and Tina knew he would always be able to thrill her, always be able to incite her need. And because this was forever, she wanted no secrets from him. His lips nuzzled her cheek, and when he spoke his breath tickled her earlobe. She shivered and then giggled, almost losing interest in what she wanted to say.

"All right, Tina," Adam said. "Talk. You know what I want—you and Holly with me." He looked down at her quizzically. "Now tell me what you want. No, let me guess. You want to quit modeling, too."

"Of course I do. You know that," she reminded him.

"But not until the campaign is over."

"Not until then," she promised. "Holly and I are both committed to Generations."

"And after that?" Adam asked.

"I'll need to arrange for repairs on the inn and put Kam and Eli totally in charge, giving them a larger share in Timberline. In a way, it belongs to them."

"I agree," Adam said. "You couldn't have better people there." They stopped for a long moment to kiss again before Adam asked, "What's the rest, Tina? What are you really getting at? And don't tell me you want to take over Century Cosmetics."

Tina laughed. "Good Lord, no."

"You probably could if you wanted to."

Tina laughed. "Don't worry, your job is safe. What I really want is to go back to school. Full-time. I can live a good life here with you in New York, but I still need something for myself. Despite the fact that Dr. Forrester is celebrity struck, he's a fine teacher, and there're many more like him in the English department. I want to get my degree—and then, who knows? Maybe even a doctorate."

"You're not kidding, are you?"

"Not one bit," Tina said adamantly.

"Then go to it, my beautiful scholar." He kissed her again, hungrily and thoroughly. When he raised his head to look down at her, his eyes narrowed in amusement. "We're going to be a rather strange family—the model turned high-school student, the model turned college student and the football player turned executive, turned family man. All of our images have shifted and changed."

"Images don't matter at all," Tina said, raising her face for one more kiss. "I've finally learned that. Nothing matters now but our love."

The kiss they shared was filled with that love; it was the first kiss of their new life together.

The Silhouette Cameo Tote Bag Now available for just $6.99

Handsomely designed in blue and bright pink, its stylish good looks make the Cameo Tote Bag an attractive accessory. The Cameo Tote Bag is big and roomy (13″ square), with reinforced handles and a snap-shut top. You can buy the Cameo Tote Bag for $6.99, plus $1.50 for postage and handling.

Send your name and address with check or money order for $6.99 (plus $1.50 postage and handling), a total of $8.49 to:

**Silhouette Books
120 Brighton Road
P.O. Box 5084
Clifton, NJ 07015-5084
ATTN: Tote Bag**

SIL–T–1

The Silhouette Cameo Tote Bag can be purchased pre-paid only. No charges will be accepted. Please allow 4 to 6 weeks for delivery.

Arizona and N.Y. State Residents Please Add Sales Tax

Offer not available in Canada.

Take 4 Silhouette Special Edition novels
FREE

and preview future books in your home for 15 days!

When you take advantage of this offer, you get 4 Silhouette Special Edition® novels FREE and without obligation. Then you'll also have the opportunity to preview 6 brand-new books —delivered right to your door for a FREE 15-day examination period—as soon as they are published.

When you decide to keep them, you pay just $1.95 each ($2.50 each in Canada) *with no shipping, handling, or other charges of any kind!*

Romance *is* alive, well and flourishing in the moving love stories of Silhouette Special Edition novels. They'll awaken your desires, enliven your senses, and leave you tingling all over with excitement... and the first 4 novels are yours to keep. You can cancel at any time.

As an added bonus, you'll also receive a FREE subscription to the Silhouette Books Newsletter as long as you remain a member. Each issue is filled with news on upcoming books, interviews with your favorite authors, even their favorite recipes.

To get your 4 FREE books, fill out and mail the coupon today!

Silhouette Special Edition®

Silhouette Books, 120 Brighton Rd., P.O. Box 5084, Clifton, NJ 07015-5084

READERS' COMMENTS ON
SILHOUETTE INTIMATE MOMENTS:

"About a month ago a friend loaned me my first Silhouette. I was thoroughly surprised as well as totally addicted. Last week I read a Silhouette Intimate Moments and I was even more pleased. They are the best romance series novels I have ever read. They give much more depth to the plot, characters, and the story is fundamentally realistic. They incorporate tasteful sex scenes, which is a must, especially in the 1980's. I only hope you can publish them fast enough."

S.B.*, Lees Summit, MO

"After noticing the attractive covers on the new line of Silhouette Intimate Moments, I decided to read the inside and discovered that this new line was more in the line of books that I like to read. I do want to say I enjoyed the books because they are so realistic and a lot more truthful than so many romance books today."

J.C., Onekama, MI

"I would like to compliment you on your books. I will continue to purchase all of the Silhouette Intimate Moments. They are your best line of books that I have had the pleasure of reading."

S.M., Billings, MT

*names available on request